TAKING TEA

TAKING TEA

The Essential Guide
to Brewing, Serving, and
Entertaining with
Teas from Around
the World

Andrea Israel
with Original Recipes
by Pamela Mitchell

Weidenfeld & Nicolson
New York

A FRIEDMAN GROUP BOOK

Copyright © 1987 by Quarto Marketing Ltd.
Copyright © 1988 by Michael Friedman Publishing Group, Inc.

Published by Weidenfeld & Nicolson, New York
A Division of Wheatland Corporation
841 Broadway
New York, NY 10003-4793

ISBN 1-55584-051-5

Library of Congress Cataloging-in-Publication Data

Israel, Andrea.
Taking tea.

Includes index.
1. Afternoon teas.   2. Tea.   I. Title
TX736.I77 1987   642'.4   86-23345

TAKING TEA: The Essential Guide to Brewing, Serving, and Entertaining with Teas from Around the World
was prepared and produced by
Michael Friedman Publishing Group, Inc.
15 West 26th Street
New York, New York 10010

Art Director: Mary Moriarty
Designer: Liz Trovato
Photo Editor: Susan M. Duane
Production Manager: Karen L. Greenberg

Typeset by BPE Graphics, Inc.
Color separations by Hong Kong Scanner Craft Company Ltd.
Printed and bound in Hong Kong by Leefung-Asco Printers Ltd.

First Edition 1987

10 9 8 7 6 5 4

DEDICATION

To S.O.I., whose creativity and exemplary cooking
have always been an inspiration.

ACKNOWLEDGMENTS

I would like to thank the following people for their invaluable help in making this book possible: Carolyn Chris, our exceptional recipe tester and close friend; Marguerite Joppich, Susan Israel, and Phyllis Balderstone for their recipe ideas; Robin Prestage of the British Tourist Authority for his generous assistance in research; Donald Weiderecht at the Tea Council of the U.S.A. for his helpful information; my patient editor Louise Quayle; and my friends who put up with me while I was consumed with tea lore.

CONTENTS

Introduction
page 9

Chapter Three
BRITISH TRADITION

Chapter Four
INTERNATIONAL SELECTION

Chapter Five
TEA SERVICES AND ACCESSORIES

Appendices

Index

Introduction

When the girl returned, some hours later, she carried a tray, with a cup of fragrant tea steaming on it; and a plate piled up with very hot buttered toast, cut thick, very brown on both sides, with the butter running through the holes in it in great golden drops, like honey from the honeycomb. The smell of that buttered toast simply talked to Toad, and with no uncertain voice; talked of warm kitchens, of breakfasts on bright frosty mornings, of cosy parlour firesides on winter evenings, when one's ramble was over and slippered feet were propped on the fender; of the purring of contented cats, and the twitter of sleepy canaries. Toad sat up on end once more, dried his eyes, sipped his tea and munched his toast, and soon began talking freely about himself, and the house he lived in, and his doings there, and how important he was, and what a lot of his friends thought of him.

—*The Wind In The Willows* by Kenneth Grahame

Taking Tea is a celebration of the traditions, new ideas, and international styles and tastes that are harmoniously blended in the tea ceremony. "Taking tea" means something different to everyone, each country having its own history and folklore associated with tea. For my part, drinking tea is intertwined with special memories and meanings. My earliest memory of tea is of being comforted by my parents with a mug of Earl Grey with milk and sugar, and perhaps a cookie at my bedside, after being awoken by a nightmare. The warm drink was as reassuring as the goodnight kiss and the light in the closet that kept away the monsters I'd imagined to have crept about my pillow. Tea is associated with good times, too. We always had it on cold winter days or after a chilling ocean swim in the summer.

Getting to know tea requires a knowledge of the many types of tea and of the proper brewing and serving methods. In Chapter Two I have included a selective listing of the most available tea types, described their taste, and how they should be served. Just for fun, I've also explained how to taste tea like a professional, a ritual as involved as any enophile's event. In Chapter Three I've highlighted a few of the many types of tea ceremonies in the United Kingdom; some are as formal as the quintessential sterling-silver service while others are as casual and relaxed as the children's nursery set with stuffed animals and storybook friends.

In my travels around the world I was surprised to learn that tea can be served quite differently from the English way of doing it. Teas range from the thick, syrupy mint tea of Tunisia to the Caribbean setting with its African and South American influenced food. Chapter Four is dedicated to the many ways tea is prepared and served around the world. Even though you may not travel to Morocco for the real thing, all the teas here can be re-created at home or used as springboards for planning your own tea.

The original recipes created for this book are intended to serve as samples of each nation's indigenous fare. Each recipe has been given an unusual twist, while using ingredients that represent that country's cuisine. I've made additional suggestions in the text for traditional tea foods that can be made at home or bought at a specialty store or bakery, and have listed mail-order sources in the back of the book. You can use *Taking Tea* as a reference book, but true tea lovers can simply use this book as an epicurean dream guide while curled up by a fire with a mug of their favorite tea.

Chapter One
THE HISTORY AND TRADITION

Tea is taken around the world and its influence spans cultural as well as economic boundaries. Tea has played a vital role in world politics, wars, literature, romance, and cuisine. It has been ascribed a spiritual and mystical connection to the soul in the East, while in the West it has been considered in turn to be an evil liquor, a medicinal cure for almost any ailment, and a symbol of imperial oppression. To many, tea is the nectar of life.

Tea in China

Ancient Chinese character writing proclaims China the Eden of *Camellia sinensis,* the tea shrub. In the province of Canton tea is called *ch'a* (pronounced "cha") and that is how it is known in the East. From the Amoy dialect the Western world adopted T'e, now pronounced "tee." An ancient Chinese dictionary—the *Erh Ya* (350 A.D.)—contains the earliest reference to tea, but it wasn't until 800 A.D. that tea's specific cultivation, brewing, and serving methods were discussed in Lu Yu's *Ch'a Ching,* affectionately referred to as the "Tea Bible."

The origin of tea is enveloped in as many stories and myths as the tea itself has subtle flavors and colors. By one account, Shen Nung, a Chinese ruler of the early twenty-eighth century B.C., is credited with the discovery of tea. He heated some water over a camellia bough and when the leaves accidentally blew into his kettle, he brewed and tasted the pale yellow liquor. The emperor was pleased and subsequently wrote, "Tea gives one vigor of body, contentment of mind, and determination of purpose when taken over a long period of time." He even went so far as to say that it is far better to drink tea than indulge in wine, which loosens the tongue. No doubt the sixth-century A.D. Indian prince Bodhidharma, who is central to another legend of the discovery of tea, agreed. It is said that he couldn't keep his eyes open while meditating to become a Buddhist priest. Disgusted with himself, he cut off his eyelids and threw them to the ground. From his lashes the camellia plant sprouted. Regardless of who tasted it first, both

Shen Nung and Bodhidharma would be pleased to know that tea has remained one of the world's favorite drinks, second only to water.

Early Chinese tea propagators hand-picked the most tender leaves from plants that usually were grown on hillsides near Buddhist temples.

During the T'ang Dynasty (618–906 A.D.), Buddhist and Taoist monks cultivated tea for its spiritual significance. It was during this period that Lu Yu wrote *Ch'a Ching*, which was the basis for an entire philosophy of tea that had its roots in Taoism. Tea was called the "Jade Queen" and was symbolic of the mysteries of the universe. Prepared in a brick form, it was also used as a type of currency. To drink it, people used blue-glazed vessels and sometimes flavored the broth with dates, onions, peppermint, lotus, or orange blossoms. However, generally it was preferred lightly brewed, plain, and taken for a calming effect in a tranquil and meditative atmosphere.

With the Sung Dynasty (960–1279)—tea's romantic period—the tea leaf gave the drinker a sense of yin and yang, light and dark, day and night. Teabricks were discarded and tea leaves were ground to a fine powder, called whipped tea, to make a frothy drink. The cups were wider, saucerlike, and made of darker blue, purple, and brown ceramics.

Tea was introduced to the West during the Ming Dynasty (1368–1644), when it was prepared by steeping leaves in hot water. Teacups fashionable during this period were light porcelain in shades of white that enhanced the color of the brew.

In the modern world tea was one of the major factors in East and West relations. By the 1800s England had become addicted to tea, but China had lost interest in trading with the British and refused to accept anything other than silver bullion for the leaf. The British had a limited source of silver, and they resorted to trading opium to the Chinese for the very silver they had just traded for tea so that they could in turn trade back the silver for more opium. A vicious cycle continued until the Chinese emperor finally banned opium trade. As a result, opium and tea smugglers dominated trade until the Opium War (1839–1842) between England and China, which forced China to sign a treaty accepting free trade.

Unfortunately for China, England would soon cultivate its own tea production in India, leaving China the vanquished party in a competitive world.

Steamed green gunpowder tea was—and still is—hand-rolled into balls during the drying process.

Tea in Japan

Japan's tea ceremony is a mystical experience intrinsic to the Japanese culture. The islands adapted both Buddhism and its priestly affection for tea early in the ninth century when the Buddhist monk Kukai brought tea seeds home and introduced the Chinese method of brewing. But, it wasn't until the twelfth century, when the priest Eisai planted the seeds in Japanese soil, that tea was adopted as a way of life. The seeds were originally cultivated at Buddhist temples, and tea became the favorite beverage of court nobles who drank it for medicinal purposes. Soon the upper classes, samurai, and Buddhist clergy had acquired a taste for the drink. By the fourteenth century, tea gatherings were an integral part of Japanese life.

In Buddhist temples "Tocha," the game of the samurai, tested a young warrior's knowledge of the taste of different teas; in villages tea was sold on the streets; the Shogun—the military dictators who ruled Japan from the twelfth to nineteenth centuries—retained tea masters who developed the tea ceremony. Rival factions in Japan disagreed over whether or not the tea ceremony is a simple function or an elaborate affair. Initially there was a lavish, formal tea gathering for the aristocracy and royalty. It was an excuse to display precious and expensive tea utensils collected by the wealthy warlords. But by the ninth century Sen Rikyu was the Imperial tea master, and he devised a tea known as "wabi cha," or the tea of quiet taste. It was simple, austere, and required a humble reverence for tea and life. However, it did not

appeal to the emperor who preferred a glittering, exhibitionist affair. Because of this difference in taste, Sen Rikyu was commanded to commit suicide. He complied, but wabi cha continued to be practiced by a band of loyal followers. In the seventeenth century the Urasenke, Omote-Senke, and Mustizno-Koji-

Senki schools were founded to teach Sen Rikyu's way of tea. They still exist today.

Nineteenth-century Japan struggled to modernize after its 250-year isolation from the Western world ended, and the concept of the tea ceremony underwent serious changes. Many tea masters lost their status because the tea ceremony was associated with the feudal age. But the Grand Master of the Urasenke tea school convinced the Imperial rulers that tea instilled the necessary obedience and balanced order essential to modern Japan's way of life. Thus tea became increasingly popular among the working classes. By the end of the 1800s, women, businessmen, and families practiced the ceremony at home. Tea schools flourished. In 1906 Kakuzo Okakura wrote *The Book of Tea* in the United States, and both Eastern and Western societies began to understand that they shared a mutual love for the drink. Tea was acknowledged as a custom transcending language and culture.

Susan M. Duane

Left: *Tea drinking was a part of daily life for the Japanese aristocracy and wealthy warlords.*

Above: *Elaborate lacquered tea chests and baskets like these were utilized to ship tea to the West.*

Tea Meets West

During the eighth century, tea was introduced to Western countries via the Persian caravan routes. Nomads planted tea bushes in Assam, Burma, South China, and Siam, and they traded tea for cloth, glass, crystal, and jade. By 850 A.D. the Arabs had sipped ch'a. In the second half of the sixteenth century the Venetians had written about tea, the Portuguese had tasted it, and the English were told about the herb by Dutch seamen.

By the mid-1600s, coffeehouse keeper Thomas Garway in England was advertising tea as a tonic for "Headache, Stone, Gravel, Dropsey, Scurvy, Sleepiness, Loss Of Memory, Looseness Or Gripping Of The Guts..." Shen Nung, whose philosophy of tea centered around "contentment of mind and determination of purpose," would not have recognized his own brew. Indeed, the East's spiritual philosophy was filtered out of the Western cup, but the West soon shared the East's love for the cup, if only in terms of the amount consumed.

Tea reached Russia in 1618, but it wasn't until Peter the Great built St. Petersburg in the seventeenth century—his window to the Western world—that the Russian aristocracy enjoyed English-style tea ceremonies even before the British made it a part of their culture. There were lavish parties at which society women drank tea as their male companions downed cold vodka. But Russia could not trade directly with China, and tea became expensive and difficult to obtain. It was not until the eighteenth century that Russia established a caravan route and a new trading frontier. Three hundred camels would journey for sixteen months from Moscow to Usk Kayakhta (a neutral zone between Russia and China) and back, bringing tea to the Russian aristocracy. Czarina Elizabeth encouraged tea's popularity by establishing her own private caravan. During this time the Russian samovar was invented. This hot water urn was designed along the lines of the Mongolian firepot, and is still used today.

Though these nineteenth-century Russian peasants lived with hardship, at least they could depend upon the warmth of the samovar.

By the early seventeenth century the Dutch East India Company was importing tea from Java, and the drink's virtues were a topic of hot debate in Continental Europe. Tea became a fashionable and expensive commodity in The Hague. A certain Dr. Botenkoe advised the Dutch to drink ten cups daily, and saw no harm in consuming a couple of hundred. On the other hand, a Dr. Simon Paulli wrote that tea "hastens the death of those that drink it, especially if they have passed the age of forty years." An estab-lished member of the French medical profession declared that tea was "the impertinent novelty of the century." Novelty or not, by the eighteenth century tea had become the muse of many artists. The elderly French dramatist Racine, for example, drank tea with his breakfast. However, for the French and Germans, tea could not compete with the fermented grape or malted barley. Tea lost out in favor of wine and beer on the Continent, though the British Isles soon held "a cuppa" as dear to their hearts as the Union Jack.

When the British colonized India, they insisted upon maintaining their culinary protocol and decorum.

Tea in England

Although it is hard to imagine English citizens turning up their noses at tea, there was a time when the drink was considered distasteful and unhealthy. In addition to provoking controversy over its medicinal and moral influences, tea was highly taxed and became a symbolic vehicle for those at odds with the Crown. Nonetheless, Queen Elizabeth I saw tea as a potentially profitable investment. She chartered the Honorable East India Company in 1600 and granted it a monopoly of trade in the East. For over 250 years the company was a crucial player in the dramatic rise and fall of the British colonial empire.

The joy of Gift giving has for over 200 years been associated with the House of Twinings

A Casket of Twinings fine tea will be as welcome this Christmas as on any of the occasions we have suggested herein

FAMOUS SINCE 1706

Courtesy of R. Twining & Company, Ltd.

Courtesy of R. Twining & Company, Ltd.

Tea became an obsession of seventeenth-century England. King Charles II collected finely crafted tea cups, bowls, saucers, trays, and caddies in pewter, silver, and pottery. The queen introduced tea as a breakfast drink to replace ale. The notion that tea could accompany food was reprehensible to some. But certain plebian drinkers added salt, spices, and eggs. The completely uninformed chewed on the leaves. It wasn't until Anna, Duchess of Bedford, devised a ceremony of tea food in the mid-eighteenth century that tea cuisine became a British institution. One weary day at Belvoir castle, five o'clock rolled around and Anna's familiar ducal hunger pangs gurgled and growled. The Duke was out hunting, which meant dinner would be delayed. She proceeded to entertain her famished friends with cakes, pastries, and a pot of tea.

By the end of the seventeenth century tea was England's national drink. Coffeehouses should have been renamed teahouses. Queen Anne drank such massive quantities that she opted for a large, bell-shaped teapot instead of the dainty china ones popular in her day. Tea gardens at Ranelagh, Vauxhall, and Marylebone flourished, where the drink inspired friendship and became the quintessential place for romantic interludes.

Until this time, China had been England's sole source for tea. When the East India Company discovered the native Indian tea plant in the early eigh-teenth century, however, they became obsessed with growing Chinese tea in the fertile soil. China was not about to divulge the propagation and drying methods that had been dutifully kept within the confines of the Great Wall. A penalty of death was the price paid for even mentioning roasting and drying.

Indian tea representatives repeatedly told the company that the native herb was worthy of all the tea in China, but the East India Company stubbornly insisted on planting the Chinese seeds. As far as they were concerned, opium was the only Indian bud with value. Robert Fortune was hired to disguise himself as a native Chinese and decipher the secret to a cup of ch'a. He managed to get into China's plantations and returned with a knowledge of tea preparation, seeds, tools, 12,000 plants, and Chinese workers. When it was finally discovered that India's soil was not conducive to growing China tea, the secrets unearthed by Fortune were successfully applied to the native Indian plant. India became the new frontier. Tea fever took hold of British citizens the way the gold rush created frenzied get-rich-quick schemes in America.

There were those who warned against tea's unhealthy, sinful, or morally pernicious properties. People publicly debated the drink's characteristics. The Crown decided that anything commanding such attention deserved a higher tax, and this led to massive smuggling, counterfeit, and inferior tea. When a puritan writer wrote that tea was a diabolical drink, the tea debate made headlines. Dr. Samuel Johnson came to the herb's defense. He professed to be "a hardened and shameless tea-drinker." Finally, by the end of the seventeenth century, the tax was slashed and the debates subsided.

By the end of the nineteenth century the East India Company had produced 170.5 million pounds of tea, three-quarters of which kept the English busy boiling water.

Far left: *For 250 years Twinings has successfully promoted their fine teas. Their shop, called the Golden Lion, is still at its original location in London.*

Left: Camellia sinensis, *the tea plant, known as* ch'a *or* t'e *in the East, can grow up to forty-feet high in the wild but is pruned on plantations and picked when three to four feet tall.*

America's Grand Tea Party

Peter Stuyvesant brought tea with him to New Amsterdam and Dutch colonists gave fashionable tea parties where they flavored their brew with saffron, peach leaves, and sugar. But it was the English who gave tea a place in the New World's society. The colonists tried to replicate England in New York by building tea gardens like those in London. At teatime vendors shouted to passersby that they had access to the purest tea water, which was pumped from springs in lower Manhattan. But there were still those new Americans who were unfamiliar with the tea leaf. Their dislike of the brown brew probably stemmed from the fact that it was stewed for two or three hours. Some tried to serve it like spinach with salt and butter, others ate it on toasted bread. The Society of Friends (or Quakers), however, sanctified tea as "the cups that cheer but not inebriate." By the time the American Revolution began, tea was drunk by soldiers, early settlers, and in the woods by trappers. It was taken in the highest social circles, and Native Americans traded it for liquor.

When Westminster Parliament levied duty on tea, the American colonists cried out against taxation without representation. Tea became a political symbol for liberation. The irate colonists boycotted the East India Company, purchased tea from Dutch smugglers, and drank substitutes of infused leaves and roots. Many of today's herbal teas were devised during this period. Dried raspberry vine, dubbed "Liberty Tea," was consumed more for patriotic duty than potable pleasure. Labrador tea was a robust combination of various roots. Ribwort, sage, currant, and loose strife found their way into many early American teapots, replacing the camellia.

In 1773, despite many overt threats and protests from the colonists, the East India Company decided to force their surplus of tea on the Americans. The Sons of Liberty secretly met to decide how they would convince the British that they wanted neither their tea nor their tax. It was John Rowe who asked, "Who knows how tea will mix with the salt water?" Samuel Adams was chosen to lead a group of men shrouded in blankets, with lampblack painted on their faces, onto the decks of the ships in the harbor. For three hours they swung hatchets at the tea chests, then dumped them in the shallow port. The Boston Tea Party, as it came to be known, was only one of several demonstrations against tea, which soon became a victim of guilt-by-association because of its relationship with England.

While the American Revolution did little for the good name of tea, the newly formed United States decided to give the leaf another chance. America's interest was proprietary, however, as trading in tea was seen to be a boon to this new country. They built their own merchant ships, and the first such seafaring vessel proudly waved the Stars and Stripes above a cargo of ginseng to be traded for Chinese tea.

Americans then developed the Yankee Clipper ship to be the first and fastest to reach the Far Eastern shores. The boats were thin and light with masts carrying acres of billowing sail. In the early

1850s, *The Stag Hound* was the first clipper to run from Canton to New York—and did it in an unheard of eighty-five days. *Flying Cloud* was the second lady to take to the seas in the mid-nineteenth century; she ventured around Cape Horn to San Francisco in little more than twelve and a half weeks. Her sailing record is currently unbeaten. These ships were tightly packed, their narrow hulls jammed with chests of precious tea cargo. They were the regal rulers of the white-capped seas.

The English developed their own clipper, the *Cairngorm*, to compete with America's Eastern trade. The tea races that followed between 1850 and 1860 captured the enthusiasm of the public on both sides of the Atlantic. Romance and adventure became indelibly associated with the great ships as records were set, broken, and reestablished. However, when the Suez Canal opened in 1869, steamships became more economical for transporting goods. The magnificent clippers, so full of power and beauty, were relegated to carrying less important cargoes. The proud adventurers became obsolete.

The Sons of Liberty raided the three East India Company ships—the Dartmouth, Eleanor, *and* Beaver— *anchored in Boston harbor on December 16, 1773 as a protest against that familiar revolutionary cry, "No taxation without representation." All in all, 342 boxes of tea were dumped into the water, making tea a symbol of British oppression. As a response to the colonists' "tea party," the Crown closed the port until the East India Company was reimbursed for its loss. Americans' response, in turn, was the formation of the First Continental Congress in 1774.*

Tea Merchandisers and Inventions

During the early 1900s two discoveries changed the Western notion of tea. In 1904 the St. Louis World's Fair took place under a blazing sun during an uncomfortably humid Midwestern summer. The producers of Indian tea had established a booth to promote their product, but nobody bought the steaming drink until the supervisor, Richard Blechynden, poured it over ice. Customers flocked to the turban-clad men who quenched their thirsts with this new invention, and Americans still prefer their tea iced today. The second innovation that changed the way Americans would drink tea was devised in 1912 by Thomas Sullivan. He tried to interest retailers in his imported tea by sending samples in small, hand-sewn silk bags. When his customers requested more bagged tea, Sullivan substituted gauze for the silk, inventing the first tea bag.

The father of tea advertising is surely Sir Thomas Lipton who, as a young entrepreneur, marketed tea for the masses. When Lipton heard about the coffee crop crisis in Ceylon, he traveled there to buy his own tea estates. He advertised that Lipton tea came "direct from the tea gardens to the tea-pot," and undersold the market price by cutting out the middle man. He publicized his tea estates by hauling 20,000 chests through the streets in Glasgow with an escort of brass bands and bagpipers in splendid kilts. He used tea-tasting lingo to suit his own needs, such as calling his brew "brisk," which implied a crisp, refreshing taste but actually meant it was pungent. He boasted about using Orange Pekoe teas as if they were superior when in fact the name refers to the leaf size and not the grade. No matter. The public loved his sense of whimsy, and responded by making Lipton tea a popular product.

Courtesy of Thomas J. Lipton Inc.

Above and Right: *Sir Thomas Lipton was an innovator in tea advertising and merchandising as well as the purveyor of one of the world's best known teas.*

Chapter Two
CHOOSING AND BREWING TEA

To choose the proper tea, you should know your leaf. The wild tea plant, *Camellia sinensis,* is actually an evergreen tree, which can grow as high as forty feet. But the cultivated shrub, known in Latin circles as Thea Sinensis, is pruned at a more manageable three or four feet. This constant attention to height insures easy plucking of the delicate leaves surrounding the tender tip.

Tea Propagation

Tea is propagated in gardens or on estates that are usually surrounded by high mountain peaks and jungles in tropical and subtropical climates. In India, tea gardens are often in elephant country where wild elephants, rhinos, deer, and water buffalo roam dangerously near the tea pickers. The tea plantations stretch like acres of perfectly trimmed, dark green lawns dotted with eucalyptus, blue-gum, and cypress trees. In a temperate air warmed to a regular sixty-five degrees Fahrenheit, with fogs, morning dew, heavy yearly rainfalls, and intermittent bursts of sun, the tea plant will prosper.

The tea plant's seeds are tended in nursery beds where they grow into six- to eight-inch plants. The small bushes are set in well-spaced rows in full sun. In Sri Lanka (formerly Ceylon), an average planted acre will have 3,630 shrubs. After three years the bush comes of age and the first growth to be picked, known as the "flush," is harvested. A properly tended bush can live for more than fifty years. There is an infamous 800-year-old tree in southwestern China, reaching an impressive sixty feet into the air. The stoic specimen still produces leaves for which tea pickers dare to climb. Generally, tea leaves are an average small-finger size, and it takes a little over a month for a leaf to develop into a shoot containing the number of leaves required for harvesting.

Tea is produced primarily in Asia, Oceania, Africa, and South America. While China once supplied nearly all of the world's tea, today India and Sri Lanka provide nearly 70 percent. Mainland China, Indonesia, Malawi, Argentina, Bangladesh, Taiwan, Mozambique, Uganda, Turkey, Tanzania, Brazil, and Zaire are also major suppliers of tea. The most recent addition to the list of tea producers is Kenya, which is fast becoming a major tea exporter. As for tea consumption, the United Kingdom is the undisputed leader. The United States seems to have forgiven tea its historic symbolism of oppression and is the second greatest importer of tea on the market.

Courtesy of R. Twining & Company, Ltd.

Lush tea plantations are often terraced on sloping hills.

The tea you drink is made either from one kind of leaf or a combination of leaves known as a blend. Some teas are comprised of the youngest, freshest, smallest tips; others are mixtures of older, larger leaves. There are approximately three thousand leaf varieties with a myriad of blending possibilities.

Courtesy of R. Twining & Company, Ltd.

Tea is picked during a flush, then weighed before being processed and packed.

TEA TYPES

The taste of the brew in your cup is a result of the type of tea leaf it is, how much fermentation took place, how it was fired and rolled.

GREEN TEAS are generally subtle, pale, and often bitter. They are unfermented and made from steamed leaves that are rolled on mats. The steaming makes the leaves supple and curtails the natural inclination to ferment. Should the leaves oxidize without further treatment, they might rot upon removal from their stems. The rolling provides a release of aromatic juices. The leaves are then heated, which puts an unequivocal stop to fermentation.

BLACK TEAS are a stronger leaf with a rich liquor resulting from controlled fermentation. The leaves are placed in a loft where they are strewn on racks for twelve to twenty-four hours to wither. Warm, dry air circulates in the room, removing moisture from the leaves. The wilted leaves are in early stages of fermentation, and as they soften they are rolled in machines, which further encourage oxidation to take place. At this point, the fermentation causes them to change to a deep copper hue, and the leaves are placed on trays in a drying machine where hot air is applied. This causes another color change, and results in a tea leaf that is dark brown with a slight reddish tinge.

OOLONG TEAS from China are a combination of green and black leaves. Oolongs are partly fermented and are stronger than green teas but more delicate than the fully fermented black tea.

Herbal Teas

Herbal teas include every part of the plant, from the roots to the stems, seeds, berries, and flowers. Some people define "true" tea as that which comes from the leaf, others claim there is no need to segregate the leaf from the rest of the plant. Many herbal teas such as saffron, basil, marjoram, and anise are familiar to kitchen spice cabinets. Some are made from fresh herbs, while others are composed of dried plants. The fresh herbs generally make a lighter but brighter tasting drink, while dried herbs are more concentrated. Herbal teas are almost always aromatic because of the distinct volatile oils that easily evaporate and release lovely fragrances. Herbal teas are described as delicate, fruity, nutty, naturally sweet, or bitter. Most are best taken plain or with a slice of lemon and a drop of honey.

Long considered tonics, herbal teas were devised by pioneer women as their families forged across unclaimed frontiers. English farmers picked wild herbs from the countryside and dried them through the winter. West Indian voodoo cults believed herbal concoctions abetted black magic. Folk remedies for various physical and emotional ailments call for herbal drinks. Native Americans introduced mint tea to the Shakers who settled in New York. Most mint teas were taken for curing stomach ailments. "Hamburger Tea" was not what it sounds like. It consisted of a combination of senna, tartaric acid, coriander, and other leaves, and was used as a laxative. The tall and aromatic eucalyptus tree, which was introduced to California in the mid-nineteenth century, provided asthmatics with relief when the long, blue leaves were boiled in water. "Balm Tea" was supposedly laced with liquor in the late 1800s by innocent parishioners entertaining the teetotaling parson who would often leave the gathering by kicking up his heels.

When Europeans drink tea, it is generally a tisane, which is an herbal infusion. Asterlike flowers carpet the hills of Italy where they make a lovely chamomile tea. In Finland, rose hip tea is immensely popular. Dried rose hips can be purchased at health food stores, but many Finns grow marvelous rose gardens and have trellised arbors with roses that provide the leaves which they then dry for tea. In Greece, herbal teas have long been used and were even used by

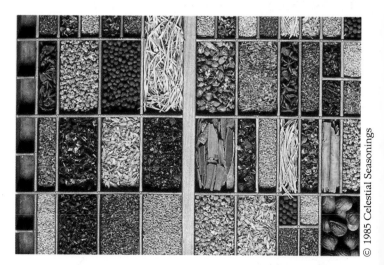

© 1985 Celestial Seasonings

Herbal teas are made from the roots, stems, seeds, berries, flowers, and leaves of various plants.

Hippocrates, who used such drinks for tonics to cure colds, fevers, and digestive problems. Today, if you order tea in a Greek taverna, you will most likely receive chamomile or mountain tea, a mixture of herbs including sage and lime flowers, best taken with honey and lemon. In France, apple, lime, and mint are popular tisanes.

South America has a very special herbal tea that you can obtain from specialty stores in North America. In Brazil, Paraguay, Uruguay, Chile, and Argentina the drink to order for those who know what to drink is maté. Made from a wild bush resembling holly leaves, it is also called Paraguay or Jesuit tea. The leaves are ground, and the powdered maté is made in gourds. It is an herbal tea rich in caffeine, and flavored with lemon or orange peel. The leaves are so potent that they can withstand two or three infusions.

Today as more and more people avoid caffeine, adventurous palates are acquiring a taste for the unusual. The sophisticated urban tea drinkers are joining the ranks of the natural foods crowd, and everyone seems to be sampling herbal teas. Thanks to this recent interest in alternative drinks, major tea companies have packaged their own versions of herbal tea blends in both loose and tea bag form. There are fruity, minty, and sanguinely soothing combinations such as chamomile with blueberry leaves and passion flower or blackcurrant. In the United States many small cottage industries are booming with sales of successful herbal tea mixtures, perfect meldings of spearmint, alfalfa, peppermint, and blackberry leaves with hibiscus flowers, red clover blossoms, and roasted chicory root. Cranberry, almond, rosehip, apple, and ginseng are among the more unusual herbal teas available.

To make your own herbal tea, it is generally best to use a well-rounded teaspoon of the herb for each cup of boiling water. Loose herbs can be purchased in health food stores and specialty shops. The leaves of herbs should be infused just like regular tea. Roots should be boiled for fifteen or twenty minutes and then strained. Seeds and berries are best crushed slightly in a mortar, then simmered in water for eight to ten minutes before they are strained and served piping hot. Here is a list of some of the flower, leaf, root, seed, and berry teas you might like to try.

Flower Teas: Chamomile, chrysanthemum, red clover, hibiscus, jasmine, lavender, lemon, lime, orange, linden, rose, saffron, yarrow and lichee are some of the dried blossoms that make fragrant teas.

Leaf Teas: Alfalfa, basil, bay, comfrey, dandelion, marjoram, parsley, peppermint, raspberry, rosemary, sage, spearmint, strawberry, and thyme are some of the most familiar leaves to grace a tea cup. There are also the wonderfully unexpected and unfamiliar ones like "Bee Balm Tea," which makes a strong and minty infusion sometimes called "Oswego Tea," and "Borage Tea," which has a surprising and unusual cucumber taste. The leaf we usually think of as a feline's delight, catnip, makes a lovely infusion. The Japanese have a favorite called "Kobucha." There are amusing names taken from plants known as moterwort or lovewage, which tastes like celery. Some leafy concoctions are mixed to taste like the tea plant. Such teas are often made with the woodruff leaf that has a haunting resemblance to the flavor of Darjeeling.

Root Teas: Chicory is similar to coffee but has no caffeine so it is often marketed as a rich alternative to the familiar ground bean. Ginseng is a dried root from the Orient which is best taken with honey or sugar because it has a rather bland taste. It is reputed to be a great cure-all for whatever ails you. Licorice root is sweet and good after a meal, and sarsaparilla has long been a tonic.

Seed and Berry Teas: Anise, celery, fennel, juniper, and rosehips are spicy and sweet teas.

Making the Grade

When you buy a tea there are a lot of factors to consider. Do you want it loose or bagged? If loose, will you blend it or use one type of leaf? If you like English Breakfast, a mixture of India and Ceylon leaves, or fancy Prince of Wales, a combination of oolongs and black leaves, you probably enjoy the subtle melange of flavors in blended teas. If Assam or Negril are your perfect cup, you have acquired a taste for one-leaf teas. There's also a lot more to a tea's name than a fanciful title. It can be a packager's exclusive blend such as Coronation Tea, a well-loved mixture like Earl Grey, or a reference to the tea growing region as in Keemun. Indian and Chinese teas are named in deference to the districts where they are grown. Indonesian teas often refer to the name of the estate where they are picked, and whether they are high- or low-grown. You can determine what kind of tea you might enjoy by examining the grade of leaf used in your favorite infusion. Grades are the industry's way of referring to the size and condition of the processed leaves. The grade is important to know because the smaller the size, the more quickly the leaf brews. The grade sizes vary according to the semantics and idiosyncrasies of the regions where the particular tea is grown. Southern China's Lapsang Souchong, for example, is made up of large grade leaves; it takes a good five minutes to make a satisfying liquor. Orange Pekoe is a grade name that confuses those who try to understand grades because it is also a packaged name. It is brewed in five or six minutes.

The two major grades are Broken and Unbroken. India, China, and Indonesia generally grade their black teas in descending order of large to small leaves: Broken Orange Pekoe, Orange Pekoe, Broken

Courtesy of R. Twining & Company, Ltd.

The tea plant is harvested when it is three years old.

Courtesy of R. Twining & Company, Ltd.

Tea is graded, packed, and then sent to tasters who decide if the quality of the flush is up to standard.

Pekoe, Pekoe, Pekoe Souchong, Souchong, Fannings, and Dust. China has an added classification of Flowery Pekoe and Indonesia has a Flowery Orange Pekoe, both of which refer to the younger leaf with the tips. The grades Fannings and Dust, while they would make a wonderful title for a Victorian novel, are quite undesirable for drinking.

China's oolongs are graded with: Choice, Finest to Choice, Finest, Fine to Finest, Fine Up, Fine, On Fine, Superior to Fine, Superior Up, Fully Superior, Superior, On Superior, Good to Superior, Good Up, Fully Good, Good, On Good, and Standard.

Green teas are classified differently in China, Japan, and India. The Chinese grade according to age and style of leaf preparation in three broad categories: Country Greens, Hoochows, and Pingsueys. All three can be further graded according to the ways

they are made. Gunpowder (which itself has nine subdivisions) is made of young leaves rolled into tiny balls. Pea Leaf is a bold, round, rolled leaf. Young Hyson indicates a long, twisted, or thinly rolled leaf. Imperial is a large, loosely rounded older leaf. Hyson is a smaller, older version of Young Hyson. The Country Greens are rich, clear, and fragrant. The Hoochows have a light liquoring and are flavorful. The Pingsueys translate to mean "ice water," a name which aptly describes the refreshing taste.

In Japan, the green teas are classified according to their processing methods. They can be Pan-fired (straight); Basket-fired (longer spider-leg leaf); Grui (curled); or Natural Leaf (porcelain-fired). Districts are also a point of reference. Grades are further ranked as Extra Choicest, Choicest, Choice, Finest, Fine, Good Medium, Good Common, and Common.

Tea Tasting

Once the tea is processed and graded it is ready to be exported. Before a tea shipment leaves a plantation, inspectors taste what will be shipped around the world. The tea is then bulked into aluminum-lined, wooden chests. Upon arrival at its destination, the tea is tasted again by professional tasters and blenders. From Calcutta to Brooklyn, men and women with well-trained palates, eyes, and noses seek to define what their nation requires in a good cup of tea and to maintain standards of quality control. Americans prefer less tannin content (which gives tea its somewhat bitter aftertaste) than the English and Australians, and tea tasters consider this factor when determining if a batch of tea from Sri Lanka or Kenya is up to par. In the United States the tasters gather in an office in Brooklyn, New York, and sample tea at a round table. In India, officials don white smocks in laboratories and take up to 120 tastes in an hour.

The taste of tea varies according to a myriad of factors, which range from composition of the plant's soil to the mood of the tea taster. The actual tea leaf boasts over three hundred chemical components, some familiar to the layman as caffeine and calcium, others quite unrecognizable yet essential, such as the oil of theol, which is crucial to releasing the tea's flavor. The actual taste of tea is dependent upon the astringency and pungent aroma, confusingly called the tannin content and commonly mistaken for tannin (of which there is none in tea). The tannin content is simply a combination of thearubigins and theaflavins. If this sounds like Sanskrit to you, try tea with milk and then without. The tea with milk has neutralized the tannin content so it does not affect the flavor. Green teas have the highest tannin content followed by oolongs and then black varieties. The tannin content also differs in accordance to the tea's origin. China's Keemun teas are low in tannin content while India's Assam teas are relatively high.

Caffeine content is often a consideration to those who suffer stress. Tea has a reputation for being low in caffeine, but it is actually higher in caffeine than coffee if measured pound for pound. The reason is that a pound of tea provides 200 cups as opposed to forty cups from a pound of coffee. This works out to three-quarters the amount of caffeine in a cup of Darjeeling as compared to a cup of Mocha Java. Black tea has three times as much caffeine as green tea, and the oolongs fall somewhere in the middle.

From a single sip, professional tea tasters can determine the composition of the tea leaf, size, height of its growth, exposure to rain and sun, and if it will mix well with other varieties. They "nose out" problems while observing the condition of the leaf, color of its infusion, flavor, and fragrance.

To sample tea the way professionals do, you'll need a kettle, a scale or means of measuring equal portions of tea, a selection of teas, cups with equal numbers of saucers and accompanying bowls, a timer, and a large vessel to use as a spittoon. Line selected teas up on a windowsill; a northern exposure is best for illuminating the tea's true color. Next to each tea, place a teacup, saucer, and bowl. A professional's equipment consists of a large, white porcelain cup with a serrated edge, lid, and a smaller porcelain bowl. If you can't obtain true tea-tasting paraphernalia, a white china or glass cup will do. Freshly drawn and filtered water should be prepared for boiling. If you are unsure of your tap water's purity, use bottled water instead.

The first stage of tasting is primarily a sensual experience for the eyes and nose. Inspect the dry leaves for color, texture, and fragrance before weighing out a half ounce on a scale. The leaves should not be blistery, which is indicated by swollen, hollow fragments. They also should not be bakey, which means they've been overcooked so that they seem brittle, lacking moisture that will most assuredly result in a taste without sparkle. If you are sampling black tea, look for a slight reddish tinge in the leaves. If it is a flavored tea, tips and flower buds should be

Buyers, blenders, and inspectors visit the importers' warehouses to weigh and sample the unblended teas.

visible. Once you've looked at and smelled the fragrance of the leaf, place the tea in the appropriate cup. Add boiling water and place the saucer over the brew for five or six minutes. Be consistent with the time you allow each tea to brew. The tea should then be strained into the smaller bowl. Next, add a teaspoon of skimmed milk to determine the true color of the tea without masking the flavor.

At this point, any of Emily Post's converts had best leave the room. The second stage of tea tasting begins when a large tablespoon of tea is loudly slurped into the taster's mouth, against the back of the tongue, which allows the aroma of the tea to be sensed simultaneously with the taste. The tea is then spat out into a large spittoon and the next sample is tasted, following the same procedure.

Today's American tea tasters use the same criteria that these professional tasters did in 1876.

Tea Terms

Like wine connoisseurs, tea tasters thrive on using vocabulary that personifies the sensual experience that drinking tea can be. If, for example, you overhear two people discussing a "mature, curly, heady-type with good body," don't assume they are fantasizing about a love interest—they might be professional tea tasters talking shop. Tea-tasting lexicon has been likened to the Eskimos' one hundred words describing snow, with nearly as many images specific to the taste of tea. However, one need not be daunted by the prospect of learning the jargon. Once certain basic criteria are understood, the rest will follow with each swirl of infusion on the tongue.

The first thing to determine in tasting is the pungency, a sharp and slightly acrid but not bitter taste. Look for body; is the tea strong and bold? Brightness is the sparkling color of the liquid which denotes good tea that is full of life. Purity is important; are there any stems or other debris? Tea's flavors can be described as delicate or bitter, robust or mild, subtle or sharp, fruity or spicy, smokey or wine-like. Colors range from green to pink, yellow, and amber.

Each tea has a characteristic color, aroma, and taste that can be identified by specific tea-tasting terms.

Brian Leatart

TEA–TASTING TERMS

Follow this list of tea terminology to help you speak the language of professionals and specify what you like, or dislike, in a cup of tea.

AGONY OF THE LEAVES: The unfolding of the leaves when subjected to boiling water.

AROMA: The smell of the tea leaf and infusion associated with the tea's flavor and fragrance.

BAGGY: An undesirable taint in the dry leaf, as well as in the liquor of the tea.

BAKEY: The result of a tea that is too high-fired, too much moisture removed.

BANJI: Two leaves without a dormant bud, sterile.

BISCUITY: The pleasant aroma occasionally sensed in the leaf or liquor of well-fired Assam tea.

BLACK TEA: Any tea that has been well-fermented before being fired as opposed to green or oolong teas.

BLEND: A mixture of different growths.

BLISTERED: Swollen or hollow leaves that carry bubblelike cavities which result from drying too quickly during firing.

BLOOM: A desirable leaf with a sheen to it, which means it is not overly processed and was carefully sorted.

BODY: A liquor with fullness and strength, not thin.

BOLD: A large leaf, which might have benefited from cutting, or a rich and well-pronounced tasting infusion.

BRIGHT: Sparkling reddish infusion that can have a copper look.

BRISK: Tea that has been well-fired, resulting in a pungent, lively taste.

BROKEN: Tea that has been broken while being rolled or cut, used to define grades.

BROWNISH: The color of tea that has been excessively fired at high temperatures after improper withering or bad plucking. It can also refer to the natural color of a tippy tea.

BURNT: An infusion that has a taste of tea prepared at too high a temperature.

CAFFEINE: The stimulating component of tea, less than 1 grain per cup as opposed to 1.5 grains in coffee.

CHARACTER: A desirable property of the infusion that allows a well-trained taster to define the origin of the tea leaf, as in, "This is the character of an Assam."

CHOPPY: Broken Pekoe.

CHUNKY: Broken teas too large in size.

CLEAN: A leaf free of debris and other grades, or an infusion of an inferior tea that does not have an aftertaste.

COLOR: The hue of the infusion.

COLORY: A bright and appealing infusion.

COMMON TEA: A thin and nondescript infusion with little flavor.

COARSE: An infusion with undesirable taste resulting from irregular firing or coarse leaves.

COPPERY: Bright, copper-colored infusion, which is the sign of a well-prepared black tea.

CREAMING DOWN: A film from the milk that rises to the top of the testing cup and results in a thick liquor of certain high-grade teas. It is considered to be a reaction of the tannin content with the caffeine.

CURLY: A leaf with an appearance of whole leaf grades, instead of twisted or wiry leaves.

DARK: A poor tea's color.

DULL: An infusion that lacks brightness and is unclear, also a dry leaf that has been improperly processed.

DUST: The smallest sifting grade that is like a powder and generally of poor taste.

EARTHY: Tea that has been stored in damp quarters and has a musty taste.

EVEN: Tea leaf that is consistent in size and once infused delivers a bright liquor.

FANNINGS: Small, grainy, particle grade often used in industrial teas.

FLAKY: A leaf that is improperly processed and is flat and fragile.

FLAT: An infusion that is not brisk or pungent, with little discernible aroma.

FULL: Substantial, colorful, and strong tea that isn't bitter.

FULLY FIRED: An infusion made from over-fired tea.

GOLDEN TIP: The orange colored tip looked for in black tea.

GONE OFF: Moldy or old tea which is not desirable because of its deteriorated quality.

GREEN: The color of an infused leaf that is not well-withered or rolled. Not to be confused with green tea.

GREEN TEA: Tea that is not fermented.

GREY: The color of a black tea leaf that has been overprocessed.

HARD: Pungent, a quality looked for in Assam teas.

HARSH: A bitter infusion common in improperly withered or immature tea, also resulting from coarse tea leaves.

HEADY: Distinctively potent.

HEAVY: A thick infusion which is strong and colory, not overly brisk.

HIGH-FIRED: Tea that is processed under high temperatures. It can also refer to tea that is dried too long and has lost flavor.

INFUSION: The liquor resulting from steeped or soaked leaves, bark, berries, etc.

MALT: Tea with slight malt aroma that is the desirable result of high firing.

MATURE: Not flat or raw.

METALLIC: Coppery taste.

MIXED: An unblended tea that is poorly manufactured with leaves that are not uniform in color.

MUDDY: A dull-looking infusion.

MUSHY: Tea that is too soft because it is packed in a moist container.

NEW: Tea that has not had time to mellow so it tastes raw when infused.

NOSE: Aroma of tea.

ORANGE PEKOE: A common, long, thin, wiry leaf sometimes containing a tip.

PLAIN: An infusion that has a dull look and sour taste.

POINT: Characteristics of a leaf that, when combined, cause a strong flavor that penetrates a blend. Also brightness and acidity of the infusion.

PUNGENT: Sharp, astringent taste. Not bitter.

RAGGED: Uneven leaf.

RASPING: Coarse flavor.

RAWNESS: Bitter flavor.

ROUGHNESS: A harsh infusion.

ROUND: Strong and good color, not rough.

SAPPY: Full, juicy infusion.

SELF-DRINKING: Unblended tea that is full of flavor, aroma, and body.

SMOKY: The smoke flavor pervasive in certain infusions such as Lapsang Souchong.

STALK: A tea with stalks in it that is usually the result of a coarse leaf and hard rolling.

STANDING UP: When tea holds its original color and flavor in a quality-control test.

STEWY: Without point.

STRENGTH: Thick, pungent, and brisk.

SWEET: A light infusion.

SWEETISH: A tainted infusion.

TAINTED: Strangely flavored tea, which may have been infected by microorganisms during manufacture or storage; a tea affected by a strong aroma from another herb or chemical.

TANNIN CONTENT: The chemical component of tea that provides astringency.

TARRY: A smoky aroma.

THEOL: The essential oil of tea.

THICK: Full, strong taste in mouth.

TIP: The bud of the tea plant.

TIPPY TEAS: Tea with golden buds, which have been harvested from young leaves.

UNEVEN: Irregular tea leaf resulting from poor sorting. In infusions it means that the leaf turns different colors as a result of uneven processing.

WEAK: A thin infusion.

WELL TWISTED: Tightly rolled leaf ideal in withered tea.

WIRY: Well twisted Orange Pekoe.

WOODY: Poor flavor that is reminiscent of hay or grass.

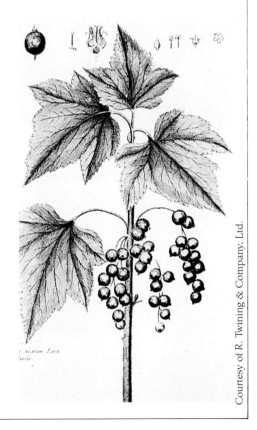

Courtesy of R. Twining & Company, Ltd.

Brewing the Perfect Cup

Even the finest tea chosen with great deliberation and precision can taste like dishwater if improperly brewed. Whether you are preparing your tea at a campsite before tucking into a sleeping bag under the stars, entertaining fifty prospective philanthropists in black tie, or devising an intimate reunion for a long-lost friend, there are a few simple steps to ensure a perfect and pleasurable cup of tea. The essential ingredients are good leaves, fresh water, and timing.

1. First, take an empty kettle and fill it with fresh cold water that has flowed freely from the faucet for a minute or two; running the water allows it to become fully aerated, providing the most flavorful tea. If the water is too full of minerals such as iron, try bottled water. Put the kettle on the burner over a moderate flame.

2. While the water is heating, take an earthenware or porcelain teapot with a loosely fitting lid, and fill it with hot water. Be sure you do not use aluminum, as it leaves a taste in the tea infusion. If you don't have a ceramic pot, a glass one will do. Swirl the hot water in the pot until the body is warm, then discard the water. Warming the pot will ensure the brewed tea maintains its optimum temperature.

3. Place one teaspoon of tea for each cup plus one for the pot into the bowl. If you don't have a strainer, use a wire mesh infuser, tea ball, or tea bag.

4. Bring the kettle to a rolling boil over a medium flame. Just as the water reaches the boiling point, turn off the flame. Do not overboil the water or it loses oxygen, and even the finest tea will taste flat. Underboiled water will cause the liquor to taste weak. Bring the pot to the kettle to ensure that the water temperature is closest to boiling. If brewing by the cup, use the saucer to cover the cup and retain the heat. Pour the water onto the leaves. Cover the pot and let stand.

5. It is vital not to judge the tea's strength by its color because some tea leaves brew light while others make a dark liquor. For small leaves such as English and Irish Breakfast blends and Assam teas, steep for three minutes. Medium leaves of Ceylon Breakfast, Orange Pekoe, and Queen Mary are best when brewed four to five minutes. Large leaves such as Oolongs, Jasmine, and Earl Grey should brew for five to six minutes. If you take your tea quite strong, use more tea. Don't leave the tea leaves in more than six minutes or the result will be a bitter-tasting drink. Gently stir the tea before pouring into the cups. You can pour through a tea strainer if you have not used an infuser. When using tea bags, squeeze them gently before removing. Generally, tea bags should be steeped for less time because they are comprised of lower grade tea, which brews quickly.

6. When serving tea with milk and sugar, there are certain rules of etiquette that stem from the way tea will taste in combination with these and other ingredients. With lemon, for example, the sugar is added first because the citric acid of the lemon would prevent it from dissolving. Milk is used in full-bodied India and Ceylon teas, while lemon complements

Tea is best sampled by following the prescribed rituals of tea preparation.

Courtesy of R. Twining & Company, Ltd.

China green or scented teas because it is said to "point up" tea's flavor. Do not use cream as it masks the tea's taste. The British Standards Institute has proclaimed that milk is best poured before the tea, though this is debated by some tea lovers. Those in favor of protocol say that the hot water scalds the milk, which brings out the tea's flavor. Samuel Twinings further theorized that the milk-first theory prevents china from cracking in reaction to the boiling water. However, Queen Elizabeth II is reported to enjoy her tea by adding the milk afterward.

One final word of warning: if your tea is too weak, don't add any tea leaves. You must begin again. If your tea is too strong, add hot water. Avoid using a tea cozy unless you can remove the leaves from the pot. Though they are often used in Europe, Asia, and Africa and are charming and ornamental, they cause the tea to release bitter tannins.

◆ GUIDE TO BUYING TEA ◆

The following guide to teas lists several blended and unblended varieties with descriptions of their unique characteristics and those particular traits that leave the greatest impression. Have fun experimenting, blending your own, and discerning what you think is a good cup of tea.

Black Teas

Name	Description	Serving Suggestion
ASSAM: Grown in northeastern India, descendent of wild tea found in the province of Assam in the 1830s. It grows best at low altitudes, and is almost always used in blends.	Bright, colored infusion with a distinct, full-bodied, rich malt taste.	Good, hearty morning tea with milk. Serve with a full breakfast of eggs and bacon or with spicy Indian dishes.
CACHAR: Product of Assam's Surma Valley, most common variety of Indian tea.	Grayish-black leaf, thick and sweet infusion.	Bright, hearty tea that is good with milk.
CEYLON: Produced in Sri Lanka, in the high altitudes of Uva, Eliji, and Nuwara.	Rich flavor, bright infusion, light golden color, pungent.	Keeps its bright color even when iced, lovely with slices of lemon. Good with Tex-Mex cuisine.
CHINA BLACK: From the Anhewi Province, a blend of traditional China teas.	Mild flavor, strong aroma of Keemun teas.	Good with mildly spicy foods, can be served with or without milk. Good iced. Nice with Thai or Korean foods. Lovely afternoon tea, or after dinner with nothing added.
CHING WO: Not often seen outside of China, it is found in specialty shops and considered the finest South China Congou from the province of Fukien.	Tightly rolled, long leaf with a delicate flavor, bright reddish color, good body.	Best served with a slice of lemon after dinner.
CORONATION TEA: A blend of India and Ceylon teas originally prepared by Jacksons to commemorate the 1953 coronation of Queen Elizabeth II.	Hearty, full-bodied tea with distinct character of Ceylon and strong taste of Assam resulting in a bright infusion.	Good afternoon tea with milk.

DARJEELING: The "champagne" of teas, grown in the foothills of the Himalayas, best picked in June and October. Gold tip Darjeeling is the cream of the crop. If tips are present it has been well manufactured.

Wonderfully delicate, full-bodied tea with a rich amber color, muscatel flavor, and exquisite bouquet. It also has a pleasant, lingering aftertaste.

Good in small cups taken plain, or before bed in a mug with milk and sugar. If preparing as iced tea, let it cool before adding ice or it will cloud. Complements Indian curries, wonderful as an after-dinner drink. Also good with a Jambalaya.

DOOARS: From a district in India that generally produces it for blending.

A black leaf, soft and mellow infusion, that has a charming bouquet. Perfect for someone who wants a tea less full-bodied than an Assam but not as flavorful as a Darjeeling.

Nice for a mid-morning or afternoon tea break, taken with a slice of lemon.

DRAGONMOON: A blend of Darjeeling and Assam teas.

Like the Dooars, but richer and thicker.

Good mid-morning or afternoon tea break, taken with milk. Complements sweets.

EARL GREY: Oil of Bergamot, derived from a citrus fruit, is the secret fragrance of this tea. Jacksons has the original recipe and Twinings offers its own version blending Darjeeling and China tea leaves.

Delicately scented, a pale, clear infusion of mild flavor. Packagers who use too much oil can give this otherwise demure drink a perfumed, soapy taste.

Best served with a slice of lemon, good with high tea. It complements fish dishes and goes well with sweets.

ENGLISH BREAKFAST: A blend of India and Ceylon teas. The name is a North American invention.

The leaf is small, the infusion full-bodied and rich.

Most popular breakfast tea because its strength makes it an eye opener. Good with milk and sugar.

HU-KWA TEA: Named for a wealthy Chinese merchant, this was also the name of America's first commercial clipper ship.

Like Lapsang Souchong, but less smoky.

IRISH BREAKFAST: Assam and Ceylon tea blend.

A strong, full-bodied tea, pungent and robust.

A hearty breakfast tea that comforts when taken with milk and sugar beside a glowing hearth. It is also good with dinner.

JASMINE: From Foochow, made with a blend of Hyson green tea and China black or Pouchong. It is scented with white jasmine flowers. The blossoms are scattered on beds of hot, just-fired tea leaves. When the buds are removed, the scent remains. Sometimes, in finer blends, the blossoms are retained with the tea.

Mild, heady flavor, refreshing and sweet.

Best after an Oriental meal, served plain either hot or iced.

KEEMUN: From China and Taiwan, the finest of China's black teas. The quality can vary from season to season. At its best it is called the "burgundy" of China teas. Sometimes it is blended into English Breakfast.

Rich, flowery aroma, full, thick infusion, strong taste, dark amber color.

Good afternoon tea or after dinner with milk but no sugar. Also good with Oriental foods.

KENYA: High-grown tea from Africa.

Tippy tea made of black leaves with rich aroma and brisk flavor. Reddish-black infusion, which is slightly fragranced and flavorful.

Good with milk. Best when accompanying a meal with poultry or game.

LADY LONDONDERRY'S MIXTURE: Named for London's famous socialite, a blend of Ceylon, India, and Formosa teas exclusive to Jacksons.

Medium-strong tea with a pleasant aroma.

Good afternoon tea, lovely with delicate cakes and cookies.

LAPSANG SOUCHONG: South China Coungou originating in Fujian Province. Sometimes blended with Assam and Ceylon.

Distinctively large, black, slightly curled leaf. The infusion is rich and smoky with a strong aroma.

Perfect afternoon tea that complements both the delicate tea sandwiches or heartier fare such as salmon or chicken at a high tea. Also, quite good on its own with a slice of lemon and a plate of simple butter cookies or drop biscuits. Can also be taken with milk. Particularly wonderful accompanying a meal.

LEMON TEA: A blend of high-grown Ceylon teas with lemon peel and essence added.

The partnering of this medium-sized leaf with citrus makes for a delicately flavored infusion with a light color.

Refreshing summer drink, good iced. It is taken plain, and if iced it should be made stronger.

NILGIRI: Translated, the name of this tea means "blue mountains." It grows in southern India at high elevations. The vintage teas are produced in December and January, but it has a year-round flush and is mostly used for blending.

Bright and brisk liquor, mellow and clean flavor, strong and fragrant infusion.

Good with lemon or milk.

ORANGE PEKOE: A grade of tea often confused for a blend, it is also a brand name for some companies. Generally a high-grown leaf.

A large leaf with flavor that varies from very delicate to bland.

The tea leaf most often encountered, it is appropriately taken at lunch with or without milk and sugar. It is an abundantly sweet, perfectly suited afternoon tea.

PRINCE OF WALES: A blend of China teas from the Anhwei Province, exclusive to Twinings.

Rich, aromatic, thick infusion with amber color.

Wonderful afternoon tea with or without milk, complements cheese and fruit desserts.

QUEEN MARY: Exclusive to Twinings, a Darjeeling blended with fine Broken Orange Pekoe, which was originally supplied to Her Royal Highness, Queen Mary.

Delicate, refreshing.

Excellent morning tea taken with milk or lemon.

RUSSIAN: Grown in the foothills of the Caucasian Mountains bordering Russia and Turkey. These tea plantations date to 1848 when they were established by the Czar.

Long leaf. Like a China tea. Thin, light liquor with a somewhat flat flavor.

Best served with a slice of lemon.

RUSSIAN BLEND: Traditional Russian combination of three parts Lapsang Souchong to one part Orange Pekoe or Northern China Coungou.

A liquor similar to hearty Keemuns with a full, thick infusion, but lighter in body.

Complements Oriental foods.

RUSSIAN CARAVAN: A blend of China black and oolong teas, said to be more flavorful because it was carried by land and not exposed to moist sea air, which lessens flavor.

Strong, dark infusion. Striking aroma of oolongs.

Good afternoon and after-supper tea, best taken with a slice of lemon. Wonderful with Russian foods such as pirogen.

YUNNAN: From southwestern province of China.

Surprisingly light and delicate in comparison to most South China Coungous. Long golden leaves are delicately twisted to make a golden infusion.

A delicate tea to be taken mid-afternoon. Good contrast to spicy cuisines.

Oolong Teas

Name	Description	Serving Suggestion
BLACK DRAGON: From China's Amoy, Foochow, and Canton provinces as well as Taiwan.	A delicate, fruity infusion with a light color.	Wonderful with fresh fruit desserts.
CHINA OOLONG: From both China and Formosa, generally a blend of 50 percent each.	Large brown leaf, gentle infusion, exquisite fragrance of sun-ripened fruit.	Lovely afternoon tea, or after dinner, taken plain.
FORMOSA OOLONG: Originated in Indochina. The yield is small, with five crops produced from April to December. The second and third harvests are best.	Astringent like Darjeeling, no bitterness.	
MAINLAND OOLONG: From China.	Often scented with jasmine and gardenia, a surprisingly nutty taste.	Complements fruity desserts.
POUCHONG: From Foochow and Taiwan. Sometimes called Pao-Chung.	Rougher than the Formosa, it is still a relatively delicate tea with a very unique bouquet.	Good afternoon tea.

44

Green Teas

Green teas are always taken plain. They are a wonderful accompaniment to Oriental foods, though they can be bitter and for some people are an acquired taste. Sometimes they are best had after a very sweet dessert.

Name	*Description*
GUNPOWDER: A grade of tea in which leaves are rolled into small round pellets. It is also a brand name. The Chinese call it Siaou Chu, and it is grown in China's Anhwei Province and Taiwan. The smaller the pellets, the younger the leaves and the finer the quality.	A clear, subtly fragrant infusion, mildly astringent with varieties that range from slightly bitter to sweet. The color is yellow-green.
GYOKURO: Also known as ''Pearl Dew,'' it is considered the white wine of teas. This is the finest grade of exported Japanese tea. It is made from the tender tips of plants grown in shaded gardens. It is treated by hand, is expensive, and, outside of Japan, is found only in specialty stores. It also has a high caffeine content.	Rich, herbaceous flavor, slightly sweet.
HYSON: Bears the name of a wealthy East India merchant who first sold it to England. The name translates to ''flourishing spring.'' It is pan-fried.	An older, large, bluish-black leaf that is hard and twisted. The infusion is fragrant, light, and mellow. It is often bitter.
IMPERIAL: A type of Ceylon, China, or India green tea.	Made from rolled older leaves after the gunpowder grade is sifted out. It results in a bold infusion.
MATCHA: Also known as Tencha. The Japanese powdered tea used exclusively for the tea ceremony.	Young leaves of mature plants are used to make this thick and bitter infusion.
PINGSUEY: One of the most prominent green teas from China's Chekiang Province. The first flush is favored. It is named for the market town where it is sold, and means ''ice water.''	A light and sweet infusion with a blue-green color, particularly with the first flush.

RUNCHI: Chinese green tea produced in this Indian district.

Medium to full-bodied tea with a brassy flavor.

SENCHA: The most common Japanese tea. Popular in Japanese restaurants in the West with sushi.

Light-bodied, refreshing but thin tasting infusion.

SHOU-MEI: China green, sun dried and minimally processed. It is known as "Old Man's Eyebrows."

Color and aroma close to that of fresh picked leaves. Bitter taste.

SPIDER LEG: Japanese tea named for the plant's long, thin, twisted leaves. It is basket-fired.

Looks like short pine needles. Thin taste.

YOUNG HYSON: A tea grade that has become a brand name. The name translates to mean "before the rains." It is pan-fired.

Young or medium-aged leaves, thinly twisted.

White Teas

These are very rare teas that are highly prized and produced exclusively in China. They are primarily from the Fukien province. They are generally taken without a meal.

Name	*Description*
YIN-CHEN known as Silver Needles.	All white teas are made from tips; their infusions are pale golden and slightly sweet.
PAI-MU-TA known as White Peony.	
YING-MEI known as Noble Beauty.	
SILVERY TIP PEKOE	

Library of Congress

Chapter Three
BRITISH TRADITION

In the United Kingdom there are many versions of the tea ceremony. Some ceremonies bear the names of events with which they are associated, such as "Wimbledon Tea"; others recall special foods known to grace the teatable, as in the "Bakewell Pudding Tea," or rooms where tea is taken like the "Dining Room Tea."

Wherever and however it is practiced, a "come to tea" invitation conjures images of much more than what is made in the kitchen. The tea ceremony is rarefied entertainment; inviting someone to tea is a custom which speaks of friendship spirited by a subtle parley of words, comforting foods, and a drink that warms the heart.

Afternoon Tea

"There are few hours in life more agreeable than the hour dedicated to the ceremony known as afternoon tea."
—Henry James

Just saying "afternoon tea" gives a feeling for the event. One's breath rushes out in the first part of the word like a sigh of relief. The remaining syllables are clipped and terse, to give the distinct impression that British propriety is tantamount to enjoying life: One can linger and relax, but one must still behave.

Traditionally, rules of etiquette are performed like scripted ritual at a formal afternoon tea. At intimate gatherings the tea-server pours the tea while seated with the guests. First the server asks, "Sugar, one lump or two?," then places the sugar in the cup. Then, with a demure smile, the server asks, "Milk, or lemon?" The milk is poured before the tea, and for lemon-takers, offer a plate upon which there are thinly sliced lemons with a small fork. After handing the cup to the guest, offer hot water for those who like a weaker infusion. Once everyone is served, the guests select from a copious array of goodies on the table or tiered cake stand. Each guest takes a napkin, which is folded on a small plate, and a butter knife for spreading jam, cream, or sweet butter.

At bigger tea parties ask a guest to serve, and don't feel as if you've admitted to being abandoned by your hired help. It is considered an honor to be guardian of the teapot, a position which implies trust and exemplary social graces. At such teas the food is best displayed on long trestle boards set with silk or lace runners, or on small side tables scattered about the room. This way, people can help themselves and sit wherever they like. If amidst the casual chatter you sense a novice participant having difficulty balancing the full cup, saucer, plate piled with cakes and sandwiches, knife, and napkin—don't worry. Dropping crumbs and spilling tea are initiation rites, part of the enjoyment of the ceremonial pomp. It reminds us that beneath the prim and proper exterior, we're all human.

At four o'clock, chimes toll the glory of afternoon tea. The British are renowned for stopping everything in deference to this ceremony. All the elements are coordinated at a formal affair, with dainty cups and saucers matching small plates. Sugar bowls, creamers, and silver or fine bone china teapots are distinguished but not necessarily matching components. The flatware is lustrously shiny silver but simple, because an afternoon tea always suggests refined and subdued finesse. At a more informal gathering, exact matches of china are less important than complementary colors and patterns. Linens set the mood. While a formal tea might call for starched white napkins, floral prints are appropriate at a less official function. Cover tables with pastel skirts and topcloths with rosebud patterns. What truly accents the smooth and demure finery is the food. Sometimes all you need are crisp white doilies for place mats to offset the lavish spread.

Teatime has come to be associated with a traditional cuisine stamped by the talents of individual cooks. Crumpets lathered with butter, tea breads

For a resplendent tea, serve cookies, jam lathered scones, and fruit tarts on a tiered service. A Strawberry Charlotte and sandwiches complete the menu.

Courtesy of R. Twining & Company, Ltd.

BULLY FOR AUSTRALIA'S BILLY TEA

In *My Brilliant Career*, Miles Franklin's charming story of a young Australian girl's coming of age, she writes about a peculiarly "Aussie" way of consuming tea: "The men boiled the billy and made the tea, which we drank out of tin pots, with tinned fish and damper off tin plates as a completion of the menu, Mr. Ledwood and I at a little distance from the men. Tea boiled in a billy at a bush fire has a deliciously aromatic flavor, and I enjoyed my birthday lunch immensely. Leaving the cook to collect the things and put them in the spring-cart, we continued on our way, lazily lolling on our horses and chewing gum leaves as we went."

The Australians are tremendously fond of a good cup of tea, and drink it in cafes near the Melbourne opera or by camp fires in the outback. When it is taken in the dry and scruffy country inhabited by bushmen, it is called "billy tea." The swagmen, as the inhabitants of the bush are called, drink their tea in a billy, which is a cylindrical tin cup with a separate lid. The tea, a wire mesh infuser, and the billy are carried in a knapsack known as a matilda. Water is boiled in the billy over an open fire, and a good amount of tea is placed in the wire ball and dipped into the boiling water. The resulting brew is hearty and taken with sugar or an occasional gum tree leaf for additional flavor. Sometimes damper bread accompanies billy tea. It is made of unleavened wheat flour that is mixed with water and kneaded until spongy. The dough is placed in a heavy cast-iron pot, then buried in the ground with hot coals from the fire. One theory as to why so much billy tea is consumed by the swagmen holds that it helps to wash down the chewy and rather tasteless damper bread.

brimming with fresh and dried fruits, dainty well-trimmed sandwiches, tall standing cakes, flaky scones, tart jams, lemon curds, and creams preside. Many of the sweets have names that bring to mind Dickensian characters such as Singing Hinnies, Wigs, Pickletts, Quire of Paper, Fat Rascals, Bosworth Jumbles, Parkins, Parlies, Melting Moments, and Trumpington Ladies. These curiously named cookies and sconelike cakes are beautifully presented when piled high on cake stands or large wicker trays lined with French jacquard napkins.

In the winter, present your tea beside a crackling fire where the tea trolley 'lords over the hearth.

Friends can warm chilled bodies as crumpets, spiked on toasting forks, are held above the flames. These "English muffins" are best eaten hot, dripping with butter, and topped with glistening marmalade or lumpy strawberry jam. A tiered plate rack holds small cookies and cakes, while larger gingerbreads and oval-shaped seed cakes are presented separately on hand-crocheted doilies decorating glass or china plates. If it's a large room, clustering potted plants is a wonderful way to add a sense of warmth and intimacy. Group small African violets around small tables. To add to the warmth, seat guests close together at a dining room table. A white, quilted

Randy O'Rourke

mattress pad can serve as a cloudlike background to hand-embroidered runners for a colorful table cover. Resplendent centerpieces of silk and dried flowers preserve the sunnier days. Try wheat-colored grasses with milkweed pods, or silver pussy willow if you use china with some color. Heads of hydrangeas spilling from unglazed pottery makes for a more rustic effect, and dried and silk flowers are also suitable. Porcelain and beaded buds add interesting textures. You can also brighten your presentation with a white, ironstone-footed bowl piled high with cheery red apples, orange or yellow citrus fruits, or winter squash and dried gourds.

Randy O'Rourke

Left: *A tea set in the summer sun is highlighted by a bouquet of garden roses.* Above: *In winter, a cozy fireside tray with an oven-baked scone can invoke a warm feeling of luxurious indulgence.*

Victoria Sponge

This cake is essential to the most elegant drawing room tea, a classic of teatime cuisine.

> 3 eggs
> 2 tablespoons sour cream
> 3/4 cup sugar
> 1/4 cup (4 tablespoons) unsalted butter, melted
> 1 tablespoon lemon juice
> 1 cup all-purpose flour
> 1 teaspoon baking powder
> 1/4 teaspoon salt
> 2 cups of your favorite preserves

In food processor, or medium bowl with electric mixer, beat eggs with sour cream. Add sugar and beat vigorously until very light and stiff. (You can't overbeat.) Beat in butter well. Stir in lemon juice.

In separate medium mixing bowl, sift together flour, baking powder, and salt. With a rubber spatula, fold gently into wet mixture until just combined. Spread mixture evenly with spatula into greased, wax-paper-lined 11-by-17-inch jelly roll pan. (NOTE: Leave enough wax paper above the shorter edges of the pan to hold onto when turning out the cake.)

Bake in preheated 350° oven approximately 15 minutes, or until cake springs back when touched in the center, and is just lightly golden around the edges. Cool in pan on rack, then gently loosen cake from pan, carefully flip pan over onto flat surface, and remove. Peel off wax paper.

Spread preserves on cake, leaving a half-inch border on all sides. Roll the cake up carefully from long side, jelly roll fashion. Refrigerate 1 hour to set, then remove from refrigerator approximately 15 minutes before serving. Serve with whipped cream or a berry coulis.

Makes approximately 10 slices.

If you lack a fireplace, there are other alternatives. In a formal dining room, try a "Drawing Room Tea." Imagine white china with a raised pattern of grapes and flowers, engraved silver utensils, and starched linen napkins tucked into matching mahogany rings or folded into fluted fans. The elegant Victoria Sponge Cake hides a tart jam filling, and petit fours can be served by impeccable caterers who carefully watch the manners of those to whom they serve.

If you can't hire the help, or don't want to play the imposter by dressing up your visiting relatives to pass them off as faithful servants, try the "Dining Room Tea." This was originally a middle-class version of the formal affair, but it is infinitely more suitable for today's home. Set the table with small, glowing candles to create a flickering firelight. The centerpiece can be a Dundee cake crowned with a circle of almonds. At a corner of the table you might position a plate piled high with flapjacks, thick oat cakes made of a rich wheat flour. Offer your guests luminescent honey in a glass bowl for sweetening the pancakes. On a sideboard you can display a dark Madeira cake or spicy gingerbread loaf. Use small embroidered linens and antique flatware. If your means don't allow for extravagant tableware, try paper doilies and stainless steel cutlery in a classic design.

Gingerbread

One taste of this tea loaf spiced by the fragrant root and you will see that ginger perfectly complements afternoon tea.

> 2 cups (2 sticks) unsalted butter
> 1/2 cup dark brown sugar
> 1 cup dark molasses or black treacle
> 2 eggs, beaten
> 2 cups all-purpose flour
> 2 teaspoons ground ginger
> 1 teaspoon allspice
> 1 teaspoon ground cloves
> Pinch of salt
> 2 ounces ground almonds
> 1 teaspoon baking soda
> 1/2 cup warm milk
> 1/2 cup dark beer
> 1 ounce crystallized ginger, minced

In a large bowl, cream together butter and sugar. Beat in molasses and eggs, beating well after each addition.

In separate medium bowl, sift together flour, spices, and salt. Stir in almonds and mix well. Fold in dry ingredients by thirds to molasses and butter mixture. Set aside briefly.

In small bowl, dissolve baking soda in warm milk. Stir in beer. Stir in all but 1 teaspoon minced ginger. Add liquid mixture to batter, stirring just until incorporated.

Pour batter into greased 10-inch loaf pan. Sprinkle remaining ginger on top. Bake in preheated 300° oven 75 to 90 minutes or until cake tester inserted in center comes out clean. Cool slightly in pan, on rack. Serve warm with applesauce or whipped cream. (NOTE: Flavors of cake come out as it sits, best served the next day.)

Makes one 10-inch loaf.

An elegant pantry tea is set near the kitchen so the food can be served piping hot.

Jim D'Addio

Tea for Two

"Tea for Two" is not only a song, but a method of courting, sharing gossip, and intimately getting to know a friend. The name comes from an eighteenth-century street hawker's cry of "tuppence a pot" (a definitely competitive price for the drink) but it has since come to symbolize romance.

The setting is intimate and cozy. Place a small table in a corner of the room, perhaps near a bay window surrounded by plants. A silk screen covered in English flowered wallpaper provides additional privacy. Telemann's "Twelve Fantasies for Flute" or Duke Ellington's "In a Sentimental Mood" will underscore messages that are passed as lips are wiped. Long, starched, white tablecloths hide feet that flirtatiously find their way up a dining companion's calf. The trick is to maintain an Edwardian sense of dignity while acknowledging the rising heat that may or may not be emanating from the tea.

A single stem sweetheart rose as a centerpiece doesn't interfere with leaning across the table for holding hands or whispering private thoughts. A silver, three-tiered stand provides service without the intrusion of a waiter. Thinly trimmed watercress and egg, or carrot and cheese sandwiches are taken from the top level and eaten from individual, small china plates. French faience hand-painted dessert plates are a nice choice, as is rose-colored glass. On the second tier of the stand, a pile of triangular and round currant, wholemeal scones are wrapped in a linen cloth that matches the eyelet-edged napkins. This keeps the scones warm for the fancifully curled

melting butter that is in individual pots at each place, or molded into a heart-shaped china dish. Chocolate, a reputed aphrodisiac, is an essential ingredient that should be placed on the bottom of the stand or on a separate cut-glass plate in the form of a

Courtesy of R. Twining & Company, Ltd.

two-layer chocolate mocha cake. It is sinfully rich, like the long-awaited goodnight kiss. Passing a plate of delicate lace cookies provides a good opportunity for hands to accidentally brush one another. And, as if there hasn't been enough, a toast rack full of lovely, golden buttered bread to be spread with fresh marmalade or quince jam, stands triumphantly on the table. Hammered English flatware is elegant, and each person might like an individual white china pot of hot water for weakening the tea that brews in a matching teapot.

The best tea for this affair is the celebrated Darjeeling, which intoxicates with its rich, full-bodied liquor. Taken plain, or with lemon, no sugar need be added. As Henry Fielding so accurately observed, "Love and scandal are the best sweeteners of tea."

Elyse Lewin

Tea for two can be a lavish, rococco affair, left, *or a time for old friends to catch up on gossip,* above.

Thin sandwiches are a simple yet constant companion to tea.

Tea Sandwiches

Make these dainty morsels on the freshest bread and use the crispest vegetables. All tea sandwiches can be kept in a shallow dish, covered with a damp towel and refrigerated until ready to serve.

Egg and Watercress

4 hard-cooked eggs, peeled and diced
4 tablespoons mayonnaise
2 tablespoons Dijon mustard
Salt and freshly ground black pepper to taste
12 thin slices whole wheat bread
1 small bunch watercress (about 20 sprigs), stems removed, washed, dried and coarsely chopped

In medium bowl, combine eggs, mayonnaise, mustard, salt, and pepper and blend with a fork to desired consistency.

Divide and spread egg mixture evenly among 6 bread slices. Sprinkle with watercress; top with remaining bread slices. Trim off crusts and cut each sandwich into 4 small triangles.

Makes 24 sandwiches.

Cheese and Carrot

1 cup grated carrots (about 4 medium-small carrots)
1 cup shredded cheddar cheese (about 4 ounces)
8 tablespoons mayonnaise
16 slices whole wheat bread
Salt and freshly ground black pepper to taste

In medium bowl, toss together grated carrots and cheese. Divide and spread mayonnaise evenly among bread slices. Sprinkle with salt and pepper. Spread 8 slices with carrot-cheese mixture. Top with remaining bread slices. Trim off crusts and cut each sandwich into 4 squares, triangles, or fingers.

Makes 32 sandwiches.

Cucumber and Radish Sandwiches

1 large cucumber, peeled and very thinly sliced lengthwise
1 tablespoon white wine vinegar
Salt and ground white pepper to taste
16 thin slices white bread
1/2 cup (1 stick) unsalted butter
1 small bunch red radishes, washed, trimmed of stem ends and very thinly sliced crosswise

Place cucumber slices in a shallow non-aluminum bowl or dish. Sprinkle with vinegar, salt and pepper and let stand 2 to 3 hours.

Trim crusts from bread and spread approximately 1/2 tablespoon butter on each slice. Cut each slice into 4 squares or fingers.

Drain cucumber slices well, pat dry with paper towels, then cut into bread-size lengths. Layer cucumber slices on one half of the bread and overlap radish circles—so that red edging shows—on the other half. Gently press the two halves together.

Makes 32 sandwiches.

Nursery Tea

"Nursery Tea" is populated less by food than by literary characters we've grown to love. It brings to mind Arthur Ransom's *Swallows and Amazons,* the tale of ruddy-faced English children braving fantastic seafaring adventures of shipwrecks and treasure hunts, where campfires were accompanied by bickies, tinned-pemmican, marmalade, chocolate, and tea. Or perhaps we think of Winnie the Pooh joining Christopher Robin, Piglet, and Eeyore for a tea party with toast and, of course, a pot of honey for our favorite bear. Mary Poppins had a way with children, and teatime often led to impossible fits of laughter causing everyone to float in the air. Even Toad took tea in an Proustian manner in *The Wind in the Willows,* and children can't help but think of Alice's adventures at the Mad Hatter's tea party where everyone changed places at the table as if playing musical chairs.

The "Nursery Tea" takes place wherever it is conducive for children to play. Set miniature tables in the child's bedroom where familiar toys and books are good company. The kitchen is another favorite location because devilish food pranks or accidents can easily be wiped clean. Sometimes, weather permitting, a grassy field invites visiting rabbits and butterflies to help create an atmosphere of wonderment. Both little boys and girls love to play "mother" (the term sometimes used in England to refer to the tea server) and pour for themselves and friends. Plastic or sturdy mugs are best, and dollhouse cups and saucers are fun for serving stuffed animal companions. Beatrix Potter plates or other elements with drawings and fanciful colors grab a child's attention. Use a small, easily managed, non-breakable pot for pouring the tea. Serve bite-size squares of cakes or trimmed finger sandwiches. Cover the table with a large sheet of white paper and set up a centerpiece mug full of colored crayons ready for drawing.

Courtesy of Laura Ashley

Invite your child's favorite dolls and toys to his or her tea party, **above.** *Using storybook characters,* **right,** *is a delightful way to entertain at a nursery tea. Here the table is set with triangle toast to be spread with strawberry jam, oven and griddle scones, jam tarts, and sinfully fudgy brownies.*

Tessa Traeger

Tessa Traeger

"Nursery Teas" are full of comfort foods, and sometimes they don't include tea at all. Lemonade, juices, and sweet peppermint tea are favorite drinks. Hot milk laced with India tea or chocolate is good in the winter. Beef tea, known in America as beef broth, is often served to the one who has a sniffle or the chicken pox, and this is best taken in the presence of a sympathetic cat or dog. The food, which is part of the child's fantasy, should be redolent and full of sounds, textures or shapes to encourage the imaginary happenings which are the young ones' version of tea etiquette. They delight to the likes of crispy cinnamon toast, mashed banana and brown sugar sandwiches, rice pudding full of plump raisins, gingermen with red-hot buttons, chocolate cupcakes capped by white buttercream frosting, and chocolate-chip domino brownie squares.

If you are an adult who occasionally feels the "over-the-hill" nostalgia for childhood, fear not. "Nursery Teas" are for grown-ups too. Have fun using big café au lait bowls with saucers to create an oversized Alice in Wonderland effect. Decorate your table with colorful fiestaware pots. This is the time to dust off your collection of wind-up toys, model sailboats, gumball machines, and faithful stuffed animals. Color is the key, and laughter is the sound effect for a fun-filled afternoon tea.

Antique toys and dolls are wonderful companions at a grown-up's nursery tea.

Banana Scones

Children as well as adults adore these biscuity treats with the surprise ingredient of a favorite fruit. You might also try adding chocolate chips.

2 cups all-purpose flour
1/4 cup sugar
2 tablespoons baking powder
1/4 teaspoon salt
1/2 cup (1 stick) cold unsalted butter
2 eggs
1/3 cup heavy cream
2 tablespoons molasses
1 ripe banana, mashed
1 egg beaten with 1 tablespoon milk for egg wash

In large mixing bowl, sift together dry ingredients. With pastry blender or two knives, cut in butter until mixture resembles coarse meal.

In food processor or blender, combine remaining ingredients, except egg wash, and blend well. Make a well in center of dry ingredients, pour in egg and banana mixture and, with a fork, incorporate dry into wet. Work dough until quite smooth and elastic.

Handling dough lightly and working quickly, shape dough into small 2-inch rounds about 3/4-inch thick. Place on greased cookie sheets and brush tops with egg wash. Bake in preheated 425° oven for 10 minutes or until bottoms are golden brown.

Makes approximately 12 to 15 scones.

Victorian Tea

The full-fledged Victorian tea is probably the grown-up equivalent of the child's fantasy spread. Queen Victoria's sixty-four-year reign left an indelible mark on English cuisine. Victoria established traditions in decorum and taste. She had two lifetime passions—Prince Albert and pudding. During her rule, coffee-houses and tea gardens became relics of the past and tea was served at home. The Indian tea leaf took Britain's fancy as Victoria was proclaimed Empress of India, and the queen's girth reflected her growing empire as well as her culinary skills.

Excessive embellishment is the requirement for setting a Victorian tea. An ostentatious wood-paneled room full of heavily draped windows and velvet-cushioned mahogany furniture would be ideal. In lieu of this, try to use fabrics of velvet and lace, and strategically place flowing asparagus ferns and grape ivy on bookshelves and mantles. Tea is presented with carved sterling silver services and plates covered with roses or other floral designs. The china ranges from majolica to patterns with bold but not brassy blues, hot oranges, deep greens, and throbbing reds. Matching teacups, saucers, sugar and cream bowls, and dessert plates are displayed on burgundy-colored tablecloths with taffeta or chintz skirts. Lace runners cover thicker table linens on side boards, napkins are frilly paisley prints with nuances of gray, rose, and plum. The silverware is shell-patterned, or has mother-of-pearl or ivory handles. Indian-style faux bamboo side tables are lightweight and easily moved to make extra room at the seating area. The Victorian love of flowers is represented by tall and impressive arrangements of dried silvery-leaved money plants, love-lies-bleeding, love-in-a-mist, and purple cupid's dart (you can tell what was on their minds). Roses surrounded by a veil of baby's breath or potted geraniums make eye-catching centerpieces. The large conch shell was a Victorian favorite, and this fascination with the sea can be

James R. Levin

further enhanced by crystal brimming with colorful sea glass. Potted palms speak of a Victorian's fantasy for far-off lands where passions can be unleashed in sultry weather. However, harpsichord music gently brings one back to the realities of the genteel and reserved English setting.

Prince Albert, Victoria, and their nine children ate teas that are robust and charming to recreate. Poppy seed cakes, almond biscuits, puddings, trifles served

Bradley Olman

Left: *For Victorian elegance, set your tea with tapered candlesticks and silver accessories; add daring to the setting with decanters of port or liqueur and place it all on a period-inspired lace tablecloth.* Above: *Tables covered with skirts and patterned cloths are appropriate for a contemporary interpretation of a Victorian setting.*

Chocolate Fig Pudding

This steamed Victorian delight combines the treasured dried fruit with a wonderfully rich combination of cocoa and ground chocolate. Use good chocolate for best results.

> 1/3 cup unsalted butter
> 1/2 cup sugar
> 2 eggs
> 1 teaspoon vanilla
> 1/2 cup unsweetened cocoa powder
> 1/3 cup ground semi-sweet chocolate
> 1/2 cup ground almonds
> 1 1/3 cups all-purpose flour
> 1/2 teaspoon salt
> 1/4 teaspoon cream of tartar
> 1/4 teaspoon baking soda
> 1 cup milk
> 1 cup diced, dried black figs

In food processor or large mixing bowl, cream butter and sugar. Beat in eggs and vanilla. Add cocoa powder, ground chocolate, and almonds; mix until light and fluffy.

In separate, medium mixing bowl, sift together flour, salt, cream of tartar, and baking soda. Add dry ingredients alternately with milk to chocolate mixture. Blend slowly until smooth.

Fold in figs. Pour batter into greased 1 1/2-quart pudding mold. Place on rack in large, deep steamer pot or roasting pan with one-inch boiling water. Steam at moderate heat on top of stove for 1 1/2 hours, checking water level every half hour.

Unmold. Serve warm, dusted with confectioner's sugar or topped with whipped cream.

(NOTE: This may be made several days in advance and refrigerated. Reheat in steamer before serving.)

Makes approximately 8 slices.

in elegant large-footed crystal bowls, and other pastries that were once rolled out by Victoria's own fingers are delightful to make even without the royal touch. Ice-cream bombes were a speciality, but you can simplify this treat by serving a store-bought brand in a cut-crystal parfait glass. The ideal cakes were molded miniatures of Egyptian temples or tortes embellished by spun-sugar flowers. A chef at the Savoy Hotel produced a cake in honor of Victoria, shaped to look like a glazed ham. You can be less elaborate but still inventive by decorating your cakes with fresh-cut flowers or fruits. Battenberg cake, sweetened by apricot jam and marzipan, is authentic to this teatime fare. Tart cherries were Victoria's favorite fruit, and are wonderful tucked into a puff pastry. The tea to have is Indian or Ceylon black taken with milk and coarse brown sugar.

Peter Paige Associates Inc.

For a formal atmosphere, parlor chairs, a velvet couch, and tea laid on a marble-topped table all create a quintessentially Victorian flavor.

Lemon Curd Bars

Lemon curd is a tart, yellow, chiffon-like custard which is taken in place of jam. It also adds a wonderfully sunny taste to baked goods. It is widely available in stores.

> *1 cup (2 sticks) unsalted butter, softened*
> *2 cups all-purpose flour*
> *1 cup sugar*
> *1/2 teaspoon baking soda*
> *10- to 12-ounce jar lemon curd*
> *2/3 cup coconut flakes*
> *1/2 cup chopped, toasted almonds or other nuts*

In large mixing bowl, cream butter. Add flour, sugar, and baking soda and beat until lumpy.

Pat 2/3 of the mixture into bottom of 13-by-9-inch baking pan. Bake in preheated 375° oven for 10 minutes. Remove, cool slightly. Lower oven to 350°. With spatula, spread lemon curd over baked layer.

To remaining 1/3 of crumb mixture add coconut and almonds. Spread on top of lemon curd. Bake at 350° for another 25 minutes until lightly browned.

Makes approximately 40 two-inch squares.

Shortbread, sesame cookies, date bars, and molded desserts are all appropriate for your Victorian tea.

High Tea

"High Tea" was conceived of in the late nineteenth century as the workingman's early supper, and today it remains the most substantial of the tea meals. It is designed to refuel the body that has labored long and hard in sometimes less than agreeable environments; it requires more than the dainty spoon and delicate cup. From coal miners to businessmen in three-piece suits, a high tea is taken for its filling but quintessentially British repast. It is best served to a crowd with a hearty appetite.

Blonde, knotty pine or any rough-hewn tables with pewlike benches or mixed highback chairs are best set before an open hearth. If you don't have access to a fireplace, use pewter candlesticks with thick candles or chunky, freestanding beeswax candles that you might ring with green ivy. You do not need a tablecloth, but woven rag or quilted place mats add a nice touch. Napkins should be rugged Indian cotton, the colors should be earth tones or, for an alternative, blue-and-white gingham. Use matching pottery, such as earthenware cups and full-sized antique spongeware. French Quimper dinner plates with crowing roosters add a rustic yet sophisticated look, or use Wedgwood drabware dinner plates with smaller brown crockery butter dishes. If you want a less rustic look, try the famous blue-and-white willow pattern, which tells the story of a Chinese maiden whose father locked her in a teahouse to keep her from the man she loved. Forks and knives are needed, a stainless steel flatware with blue handles will complement the willow plates. Ornament the table with flowers in simple pottery vases. Pick those you might gather from a field such as Black-eyed Susans, Queen Anne's Lace, Goldenrod, or deep red Sumac. If you desire a more sophisticated atmosphere, tall orange Tiger lilies, yellow Day lilies, and Cattails or Pampas Grass make a strong and lively statement of wild beauty.

"High Tea" presents an understated elegance, and the food is both satisfying and alluring. It is generally laid out ahead of time on a buffet table, which is a good way for the host or hostess to mingle while serving. The meal generally begins with a savory meat or fish dish, followed by treacle, cream, cheese, or potato scones. Welsh Rarebit, a wonderfully piquant dish which originated in the 1700s, is a savory plate of cheddar or English double Gloucester cheese combined with beer, mustard, Worcestershire sauce, and egg. It is served over toast and broiled to a bubbly brown just before eating. If you find yourself in need of an ice-breaker, the name of this fanciful dish provides good teatime small talk. People argue for hours over whether or not the appellation refers to a fuzzy, floppy-eared animal. This is also excellent served fondue style. While everyone prepares their own, they can discuss the difficulties of keeping the melted cheese on the plate. Haddock baked in milk is another delicacy. Scotch Woodcock, a creamy egg mixture served on small sandwiches spread with "gentlemen's relish" or anchovy paste, is easy to make. There are usually roasted chickens, poached salmon, baked hams, pork, or roast beef. Also gracing the table are cornish pasties, which are meat pies made in small pockets of potato dough. Hearty wheat, oat, or barley breads spill out of wicker baskets. They are sliced and served with butter and preserves, as are crumpets, oatmeal pancakes, and spiced Sally Lunn bread.

Griddle cakes with melting butter and jam or hearth-baked bread toasted over a roaring fire and covered with grilled cheese, tomatoes, and bacon are good starters for High Tea. Follow this with the overflowing platters of poultry, meat, fish, and fun desserts for which this epicurean event is known.

Seedcake

This standard teatime cake holds up well at every occasion. In this recipe caraway is ground, suffusing its aromatic flavor.

> *1 cup (2 sticks) unsalted butter*
> *3/4 cup sugar*
> *3 eggs, beaten*
> *1 2/3 cup all-purpose flour*
> *3 teaspoons ground caraway (NOTE: Use approximately 4 1/2 teaspoons whole seeds, place in a mortar and pestle or electric coffee grinder and pulverize.)*
> *1 teaspoon ground cardamom*
> *1 teaspoon baking powder*
> *Approximately 2 tablespoons buttermilk*

In large mixing bowl, cream butter and sugar together until soft and fluffy. Add eggs 1/3 at a time; beat well.

In separate, medium mixing bowl, sift together flour, caraway, cardamom, and baking powder. Fold gently into butter and sugar mixture. Gradually add buttermilk a little at a time to make a smooth, even consistency.

Pour batter into well-greased, deep 8-inch round cake pan. Bake in pre-heated oven at 350° for 50 minutes or until cake tester inserted in center comes out clean and cake begins to pull away from side of pan. Cool in pan briefly, then turn out onto rack to cool completely. Sprinkle confectioners' sugar through sieve onto top of cake.

Makes approximately 8 slices.

Next come the desserts, though they are often sampled first. The combination of apple with sweets is a British hallmark; it often appears in the form of cider and applesauce cake. Other desserts are the fancy almond custard cake known as "Richmond Maids of Honor," marmalade puddings, orange cookies called "Jumbles," mincemeat pies, the well-known seed cake, shortbread, plump boiled fruit cakes, bright strawberry jam or lemon curd tartlets, moist plum cakes, and crumbly cookies affectionately named "Fat Rascals." Indian and Indonesian teas are a perfect complement to this mixed and bountiful fare.

Jeff McNamara

High tea is usually a filling meal, but a salad with radicchio, endive, and watercress accompanied by currant studded scones is a suitable variation, above.

The English adore cheese, and pots of stilton or wheels of blue cheese often accompany teas which are also highlighted by quiches. The table can be set ahead of time with everything from the main course to the dessert and fruit, right.

Applesauce Loaf

The English traditionally use cider and apples in their baking, but this bread is unusual because tea is actually one of the ingredients.

> *3 cups all-purpose flour*
> *1 teaspoon baking powder*
> *1 teaspoon baking soda*
> *1 teaspoon cinnamon*
> *1/2 teaspoon salt*
> *2 eggs*
> *3/4 cup brown sugar*
> *1 1/2 cups applesauce*
> *3/4 cup strong, brewed tea*
> *1/4 cup (4 tablespoons) unsalted butter, melted*
> *1 1/2 cups chopped apple (approximately 1 medium apple)*
> *1/2 cup chopped walnuts or other nuts*

In medium mixing bowl, sift together flour, baking powder, baking soda, cinnamon, and salt.

In separate, large mixing bowl, beat eggs. Add sugar; beat well. Beat in applesauce. Stir in tea and melted butter. Stir in flour mixture, 1/3 at a time until just incorporated. Fold in apple and nuts.

Pour into well-greased, 10-inch loaf pan. Bake in preheated oven at 350° for 60 to 70 minutes or until cake tester inserted deep in center comes out clean.

Makes one 10-inch loaf.

Jeff McNamara

Garden Party Tea

Certain outdoor teas celebrate particularly well-loved English foods such as the Devon clotted cream or June's first harvest of strawberries. They can be as casual as rejoicing in the summer solstice, or as formal as a wedding. Most often they are simply an excuse for a romantic interlude. No matter what, outdoor teas should be served with the same respect given to the indoor cousin. It is always best to brew tea on the spot. The Russian samovar or tea urn is a graceful companion to the outdoor ceremony. If there is no other recourse, bring a thermos of hot water and tea bags.

To set the scene for a "Cream Tea" is simple. Spread a patchwork quilt or colorful blanket on the ground beneath an ancient elm or on a river bank hemmed by rows of shimmering poplar trees. To make it more formal, fresh lillies or roses in porcelain vases can grace a picnic or wicker table. Here the perishable cream can be shaded and protected from interested insects and friendly dogs (it is best to maintain a degree of reality and accept that even the most resplendent, romantic outdoor adventures are often not like what one sees in the movies). If you don't have a tree, use an umbrella table and cover it with a canvas fabric which matches pillows strewn in chairs or on the blanket. Wicker hampers with rose-patterned china and ivory-handled cutlery make for a fancy affair. If you desire a simpler presentation, try plates splattered with pastel paints, blue sponge-ware, or dark green majolica and hand-painted Portuguese fruit plates. Adorn each plate with a cluster of garden flowers such as blue delphinium, red dahlias, or yellow marigolds. For a complete picnic-style presentation, select sturdy paper plates and plastic utensils tucked neatly into a basket. Tin plates and mugs will also work well if you are really roughing it in the country. Cutlery is softened by pale yellow, pink, or blue handles. Look for stainless steel with plastic hilts. A cow-shaped milk pitcher adds a rustic, country touch.

Elyse Lewin

"Cream Tea" calls only for the famous clotted cream and some scones. The cream can be passed in a white porcelain bowl decorated by a ring of flowers, or served individually in New England goblet glasses or large white egg cups. Though clotted cream is found only in some regions of England, you can substitute whipped cream though it is not as dense. Earl Grey is a nice choice for warm weather, and Jasmine will reflect the season's abundance of flowers. Serve a lemon scented tea in a glass teapot; it flatters the fare of the garden party.

A "Strawberry Tea" is a specialty on the Isle of Wight, famous for its harvest of large, plump, juicy berries. They have been known to stain many the face of a child squatting in a field, fist full of red jewels, indulging in the joys of picking and eating fresh fruit. You might want to plan your tea after a day of strawberry picking when biting into a berry gives way to a taste best summed up in two words: sheer ecstasy. If you can, set up this tea in a field not too far from where the berries have been picked. Classic outdoor teas are often had trailer-style, taken from the back of a Rolls-Royce, where the butler unfolds a table as the maid unloads a brimming picnic hamper and china with hand-painted berries on vines. If your Rolls is in the repair shop, bring your station wagon and try a do-it-yourself version. Cover a folding table with sunny yellow or pastel-colored material, or spread a red-and-white checked cloth on the ground. Pile just-washed berries on a special china dish equipped with holes to drain wet fruit. Pure white, everyday china bowls, some in the shape of flowers, highlight the ripe, red strawberries still wearing caps of green leaves. You can also use plastic plates in designer motifs. This tea merely needs the accompaniment of scones, shortbread carried in tins, and bowls of whipped cream that are iced in a cooler. If you've planned ahead, and want to impress your guests with a knowledge of the fruit,

serve strawberry bread, strawberry pie, wild strawberry jam, strawberry sandwiches with cream cheese on date-nut bread, and even strawberries soaked in Grand Marnier and sugar, a lovely vision aptly named Fraises Sarah Bernhardt. If romance is your game, add coconut meringue cookies sometimes referred to as a "kiss," or brandy snaps in the shape of hearts to further encourage thoughts that quicken the pulse. A French strawberry leaf tisane makes a subtly perfumed and refreshing drink, or try the Lady Londonderry blend or a mint tea.

Elyse Lewin

Tea can be set in a backyard with fresh flowers and simple outdoor furniture, left, *or held in a field where just-picked strawberries can be sliced and set swimming in clotted cream,* right.

The fresh fruits of the season are the distinctive ingredients in an al fresco tea; flowers complete the setting.

Cream puffs filled with whipped cream and chocolate chips can be substituted for the traditional scones and clotted cream.

Colorful pots of flowers make the perfect centerpiece for a garden party tea.

Whole Wheat Scones

These are satisfying, flaky scones that marry well with butter, jam, or clotted cream.

> 1 cup all-purpose flour
> 2 tablespoons baking powder
> 2 tablespoons sugar
> 1/2 teaspoon salt
> 1 cup whole wheat flour (or 3/4 cup wholewheat
>   flour and 1/4 cup buckwheat flour)
> 1/2 cup (1 stick) cold, unsalted butter
> 1/4 cup raisins
> 2 eggs
> 2/3 cup whole milk or buttermilk
> Approximately 3 tablespoons milk for glaze

In large mixing bowl, sift together all-purpose flour, baking powder, sugar, and salt. Stir in whole wheat flour. With pastry blender or two knives, cut in butter until mixture resembles coarse meal. Drop in raisins.

In separate mixing bowl, beat together eggs and milk thoroughly.

Make a well in center of dry ingredients and pour in egg and milk mixture. With a fork, incorporate dry into wet and mix until it forms into a sticky ball.

On lightly floured work surface, roll out dough into flat 3/4-inch thick round. Cut out scones with 2-inch cookie cutter, re-rolling any leftover scraps. Or leave dough whole and score into 8 triangles. Place on greased cookie sheets and brush with milk. Bake in preheated oven at 400° for 15 to 20 minutes or until golden brown. Serve warm with butter and jam.

Makes approximately 12 small round or 8 larger triangular scones.

Farmhouse Tea

The Welsh, Scottish, and Irish teas are hearty displays of homebaked goods, otherwise known as "Farmhouse Teas." The essential ingredients reflect a kinship with the land: oats, potatoes, and wheat. Superstitions abound, particularly in the Irish kitchen. Stir clockwise so as to appease any specters. Cross all baked goods with a knife slash so as to release the devil. Bake Barm Brack, a yeast tea bread full of dried fruits and spices, with a ring in the middle. It is traditionally eaten at Halloween, and whoever gets the ring is said to have marriage in the immediate future.

The tea is best taken in the kitchen on a cool fall day in front of an open hearth or near the oven. You

Courtesy of Laura Ashley

The kitchen is the appropriate setting for a farmhouse tea. The table is set with pieces reflecting a rustic atmosphere.

can set the mood of Northern Scotland's Highlands by playing a recording of a lone flute lamenting the tale of Bonnie Prince Charles, or recalling the beauty of the Isle of Skye. For a Scottish tea, use mats of green and blue representing the clansmen clad in tartan kilts who "blether" for hours, which means to vociferously speak nonsense, over tea and biscuits. Or, in December, evoke a Welsh feeling by reading Dylan Thomas' *A Child's Christmas in Wales* and setting the table with muted brown pottery mugs, taupe and white napkins, and an enameled teapot. For an Irish tea, the folk music of Ireland provides the lilting accents that seem so right at a table skirted with green linen covered by Irish lace. Earthenware mugs replace the genteel teacups, bone-handled or hammered silver cutlery, or mix-and-match antique, are appropriate. For any of these teas, your center-pieces should be tall, dried grains gathered in sheaths, bowls of just-harvested fruits and vegetables, or tin tea caddies filled with dried heather and clover. A potted maidenhair fern is symbolic of the green shamrock. You might also display antique iron molds and a bread paddle to authenticate the feeling of a country kitchen.

Each region has particular culinary favorites. The Welsh adore picklets, small, light pancakes traditionally spread with jam. Their warm apple cake is delightful with cream. You might like to combine these favorite ingredients by preparing apple pancakes rolled with sour cream and brown sugar. The Scots have a penchant for oats which are included in many savory and sweet dishes. Oatcakes, available in specialty stores, are served at every table. These bland, nutty flavored crackers baffle the uninitiated, who liken the taste to cardboard. But, given a fair chance, oatcakes grow fondly on those who at first shun them, and are particularly good with cheese. Pile baskets with sweet oven scones made with currants, black treacle (or molasses), and, of course,

James Goslee III

Wildflowers are short-lived but if they are picked just before the teakettle boils, they make a lovely center-piece.

oats. The thickest, crispest, feathery-light shortbread results from a secret use of rice flour. You can have fun sampling jams on yeast breads stuffed with citrus rinds. The tongue-twisting names, like Pitcaithly Bannocks and Baps, are entertaining in themselves. Aberdeen Rowies, butter yeast rolls reminiscent of the French croissant, are popular at Aberdeen Fishermen's teas. You can easily make these at home. The Irish, whose equivalent to the Scottish oat is the potato, serve Boxty tea bread that is made in a pan or cooked on a griddle like a pancake. But, the Irish Soda Bread is the true teatime triumph. This special loaf is baked as wholewheat or white with buttermilk and occasional black currants.

Puddings are a must at a "Farmhouse Tea." Peasant Maid With Veil is a Gaelic combination of steamed breadcrumbs, brown sugar, apples, grated chocolate, and cream. The Dublin Rock put Ireland on the map as far as pudding fans are concerned. It is a pretty dessert flavored with orange water, angelica, brandy, and often decorated with greens indicating a four-leaf clover. You might try making Rood Frood, which sounds like something someone might mutter in response to an insult, but is actually a lovely combination of raspberry, currants, potato flour, and claret. A good Scottish cookbook will show you the way. Scotch whisky is never far from sight, even at tea, and it is an important ingredient in many tea desserts such as chocolate cake or Christmas fruit cakes. On a hand-thrown, glazed plate you might like to present a Border Tart that is a famous tea pastry of chopped cherries, sugar, and raisins folded into a thin shell of dough. Melting Moments could be piled high on a stand; their name perfectly describes the experience of eating these ethereal cupcakes made with rolled oats. Or, serve the traditional Northern oat and ginger biscuits called Orkney Broonies, the wonderfully tall and light macaroons whose egg whites have been whisked into high, fluffy pinions,

or darkened spicy ginger loaves more famous than the Loch Ness Monster itself.

Farmhouse fare is often marked by savory as well as sweet recipes. If your tea is served close to dinner time, try adding a smoked Haddock, grilled mackerel, or poached trout to the menu. Other popular dishes are liver pâtés, smoked duck, welsh rarebit, or the renowned Haggis. This is a gastronomic experience which requires both an open mind and a curious culinary spirit. It is a mixture of minced suet, seasoning, and oatmeal tucked into a casing, boiled, sautéed in butter, whiskey and spices, then grilled and sometimes served with cream. A tippy tea is best for this occasion, and you can blend your own mixture of Indian and Ceylon, or serve Darjeeling.

Sunflowers are lovely with old wicker furniture and woven rugs in a farmhouse setting.

Orange Marmalade Raisin Loaf

What could be more British than the tea loaf baked with the orange marmalade presented at every tea table.

> 1 2/3 cups all-purpose flour
> 1/4 cup sugar
> 1 1/2 teaspoons baking powder
> 1/4 teaspoon salt
> 1/8 teaspoon cloves
> 1/4 cup (4 tablespoons) unsalted butter
> 1/3 cup raisins
> 1 tablespoon grated orange zest
> 1/3 cup strong-flavored marmalade
> 1/4 cup milk
> 1 egg, beaten

In large mixing bowl, sift together flour, sugar, baking powder, salt, and cloves. With a pastry blender or two knives, cut in butter. Toss in raisins and orange zest.

In separate, medium mixing bowl, combine marmalade, milk, and egg and mix well.

Add wet mixture to dry mixture, stirring just until incorporated.

Pour into well-greased 9-inch loaf pan and bake in preheated oven at 350° for 50 to 60 minutes or until lightly browned and cake tester inserted in center comes out clean.

(NOTE: This loaf is excellent sliced, toasted—or warmed in oven—and served with butter.)

Makes one 9-inch loaf.

Shortbread

This is the traditional Scottish accompaniment to a cup of tea or lavish afternoon tea spread. It is often made in molds depicting the sun or thistles.

> 1 cup (2 sticks) unsalted butter, softened
> 3/4 cup all-purpose flour
> 3/4 cup rice flour
> 1/2 cup confectioners' sugar
> 1/4 teaspoon sugar

In food processor, or medium mixing bowl, cream butter.

In separate large mixing bowl, sift together remaining ingredients. Blend in butter until thoroughly incorporated.

Press mixture evenly into ungreased, shallow, 8-inch round cake pan. Score with a knife into 8 wedges; prick all over with a fork. Bake in preheated oven at 325° for 20 to 30 minutes or until cake tester inserted in center comes out clean and shortbread is very lightly golden. Cut into wedges while hot (if desired, cut carefully into 16 smaller wedges). Leave in pan to cool.

Makes 8 or 16 shortbread wedges.

OMNISCIENT TEA

If you drink your tea unstrained and try to read the leaves in the bottom of your cup "like a gypsy," chances are you won't succeed. The reason will not be your inability to decipher the cryptic message of a dampened Assam; it is simply because you cannot read tea "like a gypsy." The gypsies read palms or tarot cards (perhaps while sipping tea), but the Scottish people take credit for inventing the art of tea leaf reading. In the Highlands, the Scots rise early in the morning to read the leaves of their breakfast cups, determining if they should go about their business or get back in bed.

To read tea like a Scot you don't have to don a kilt and play the bagpipe. Simply brew loose, black tea in a pot, and pour the unstrained tea in each cup so that the leaves remain in the liquid. Once everyone has drunk all but the final sip, silent wishes should be made over the sediment. At this point, take the subject's cup in both hands. Placing the cup in your left hand, swirl it three times clockwise to the right. Invert the cup on the saucer and let the last sip of tea run off. Quickly turn cup upright again, and the leaves should be sticking to the bottom. Look for shapes in the leaves, such as animals, birds, numbers or outlines of maps, that might indicate the drinker's future. If the shapes formed portend bad luck, keep in mind that the symbols are open to interpretation and consider it a kind of Rorschach test. Turn the cup and analyze the leaves from all angles. The tea leaves are said to reflect the drinker's state of mind and semblance of daily order. If you're looking at a tidy cup, perhaps you have a happy, organized friend. Here are some common symbols and meanings:

Animals: A horse signifies ambition and success, a pig means potential children, a dog is a symbol of friendship, a cat implies chicanery, and a butterfly represents the attainment of happiness.

Objects: A ring speaks of marriage and a heart of love, clouds signify problems, anchors mean travel, ladders are symbols of success or advancement, trees offer luck, and eggs mean that you've hit the jackpot and today is your day.

Numbers: One is independence, two is opportunity or a chance to start something anew, three means travel and predestined meetings, four is stability and security, five means love, six is health, seven tells of friendship and bonding, eight will bring you impending change, and nine is a symbol of bright fortune with an added element of surprise.

A Sample Reading: You see a horse and a cat with a ring or clouds and a distinct number three. Look into the subject's eyes and, with great flair and dramatic license, inform him or her that goals for the future may be mixed with some treachery, either the treachery of another person or the treachery of the subject's own self-delusion. Add that marriage is in the air, but ambition could get in the way, and explain that the number three foretells of a meeting in a faraway place. Then look at the cup from a new perspective. Maybe you see an outline, which looks like the boot of Italy and, in the corner, is what appears to be a tree and the number seven. It seems that the number three relates to the shape of Italy, and that good luck and strong friendship will see this person through any troubles. Continue to the next subject's cup.

The classic farmhouse fruit loaf is chock full of dried apricots, figs, raisins, and nuts.

Gordon E. Smith

Chapter Four
INTERNATIONAL SELECTION

Around the globe, from Morocco to New Zealand, tea quenches thirst, revives flagging energy, and gives its every drinker a reason to slow down and reflect, engage in quiet conversation with a friend, or simply sneak a snack between meals. The drink of tea is a phenomenon unto itself, and teatime fare is as rich and distinct as the countries in which it is offered. But, while each country has its own idea of how best to tend to the little leaf, the disparate tea ceremonies are linked by a shared pleasure in a cup, mug, glass, or bowl of tea.

Exotic Caribbean

To set this tea, let your imagination run as wild as a tropical jungle. Picture yourself on an island. The pace is slow. The light is white and clear. The turquoise Caribbean gleams like a jewel, viewed from a white, sandy cove. Trade winds blow an afternoon breeze, rippling sugarcane fields, and one repairs to a verandah for a brief respite from the afternoon sun. Sharp beaked Banana-twits flit on and off the table looking for a handout. If you are sitting in the ruins of an old sugar mill, you watch iridescent hummingbirds sip nectar from the fuchsia-colored bougainvillea vines tumbling down the sides of the stone-coral building. A lizard darts away from the rhythmic footsteps of a waiter who carries a tray with teapots and a selection of tropical teatime fare. You feel luxurious, satiated by sun, temperate water, soothing bird calls, and the anticipation of an exotic and relaxing afternoon meal.

To create the complete atmosphere of this sensuous experience, you have no need to hop on a jet heading toward the equator. Your own home can be transformed into a tropical haven. Set your tea outdoors, or in a glassed-in porch or room full of greenery. Tall, potted bamboo, avocado or palm trees should be surrounding the wicker or rattan table and chairs. Blossoming orange, lemon, or gardenia plants should scent the air. Creeping vines of ivy, spider plants, or asparagus ferns can twist around centerpieces of oversized floral bouquets spiked with birds of paradise. You can also use a hollowed watermelon brimming with tropical fruits for color, or

scatter hollowed coconut shells with candles for soft light. Color is the key to decorating. Hanging bougainvillea vines are imitated by folding hot pink, green, orange, and yellow tissue paper on a string. Place a blue-green cotton cloth on the table, and cover that with a sea island batik print or use bamboo mats. Deep blue or lush green napkins can be pleated and tucked into tortoiseshell rings. At each corner of the table fill large scallop shells with sand so that the grains just spill onto the table, or prop the delicate fan coral in a bowl with small purple and pink angel wing shells. The elements are simple: use earthenware glazed in bright colors with geometric patterns, or stark white china plates to recreate the effect of the brilliant light and white-washed walls one finds in island homes. Bone-handled flatware and ceramic teapots are best. Gently whirling ceiling fans will blow trade-wind-like breezes, or hammocks and gauzed netting can be hung above the table for a dramatic touch. If you know of a friendly parrot who would keep a watchful eye on the festivities (perhaps with a running, squawking commentary), by all means pull out a bird stand. Otherwise, use prints that feature feather patterns or exotic flowers and sea shells. Play recordings of steel drums, reggae, or calypso music to echo the pulsating beat of the colorful setting.

The food should be colorful and spicy, and should reflect the abundance of fruit in the tropical trees, and fish along the tropical shores. In a wicker basket you can offer a sampling of breads made of banana, coconut, corn, pumpkin, cassava, and sweet potato. Fried plantains nestled in small bowls are good for nibbling while the tea brews. In glass cups guava jelly, marmalade, and mango jam wait to be served on toast. Lemon custard tarts and freshly made coconut-nutmeg candy are festive. Fresh fruit kebabs or salads made of ripe orange-red mango, star-shaped carambola, tiny yellow bananas, grapefruit-like ugli fruit, and the yellow-orange paw-paw or papaya are wonderful sprinkled with confetti-like shredded coconut, lime juice, and rum. Fresh ground ginger spices golden brown cakes. "Plantain Temptation" is a delicious Puerto Rican tea treat made of ripe yellow plantains baked in butter and brown sugar with candied fruit rind.

A Caribbean tea is enhanced by bright, colorful patterns and centerpieces of fruit crowned by pineapples.

TEA IN THE TROPICAL ISLANDS

When Europeans first sampled tea, it was already being used in the Caribbean as an herbal remedy and for voodoo practices. Religious cults were making tea from bark and berries to use in ritualistic revenge against enemies or to cure the hopelessly ill. Bones were taken from graves and boiled with the herbal infusions. Midnight tea baths were suggested to young women who wanted to marry; they were told to sponge themselves in sea water infused with horehound, limes, olive bush, sousop leaves, honeysuckle, guava, sage, and lemon grass.

As a drink, tea is as loved in the Caribbean as it is in Britain. Jamaica's dandelion tea is considered to be good for bodily ailments. In Puerto Rico, orange leaf tea is made from the youngest leaves and most tender blossoms of the bud, which are boiled in water for three minutes and then taken with sugar and milk. Ginger root is used to make a hot and peppery tasting drink, while cinnamon and fresh ground nutmeg are used to spice Indian black tea.

A Caribbean-style "High Tea" is full of the freshest seafood and island dishes spiced with local herbs. Serve a grilled or deep fried flying fish (or sea bass) with coucou which is a mixture of cornmeal and okra. Dolphin fish, red snapper, king fish, conch, and crab are other traditional seafoods. Some are grilled and served with lime, while turtle pie and sea eggs are rare delicacies you might find catered by those who specialize in Caribbean fare. "Pudding & Sage" is a delightful dish which is unusual and therefore appropriate to an exotic, savory tea. It is a sausage stuffed with sweet potato and spices, served with boiled pigs feet marinated in lime and hot peppers. You can make a variation by tucking sweet potato slices in bacon and serving this with a lime-juice and pepper puree sauce. Or, prepare a sweet papaya melange to accompany chicken. Deep-purple tamarillo chutney or pickled breadfruit are wonderful condiments. Plantain-egg cakes, stuffed and baked Dutch cheese, and cooked cornmeal are also featured at High Tea. If you make up your own menu, remember that "fresh" is the key word for dishes incorporating fruit or seafood. The best teas to serve are those with fruit and spice blends, or flower teas like Jasmine. You might enjoy buying fresh sugarcane and cutting off a piece for dipping into each cup.

Judd Pilossof

Tim Street-Porter

Set a Caribbean tea where sunlight, plants, and fruit create a tropical mood, above.

Papaya (Mango) Coconut Bread

The fruits of the islands burst with flavor in this Caribbean quick bread.

> 1 cup raisins
> 4 tablespoons rum, or substitute Bourbon
> 1/2 cup (1 stick) unsalted butter, softened
> 1/2 cup sugar
> 1 egg, slightly beaten
> 1/3 cup milk
> 1 cup crushed papaya or mango (about 1 large
>   papaya/mango, peeled, pitted and crushed in
>   bowl with back of spoon)
> 2 cups all-purpose flour
> 1 teaspoon baking powder
> 1 teaspoon baking soda
> 1/2 teaspoon salt
> 1 cup unsweetened coconut flakes

In small bowl, combine raisins and rum and let stand at least 30 minutes, or up to several hours, stirring occasionally.

In large mixing bowl, cream together butter and sugar until light and fluffy. Beat in egg, milk, papaya and the raisin and rum mixture.

In separate, medium mixing bowl, sift together flour, baking powder, baking soda, and salt. Stir in coconut. Mix dry ingredients into wet ingredients, beating until batter is thoroughly blended.

Spread mixture evenly in greased 9-inch loaf pan and bake in preheated oven at 350° for 1 hour or until cake tester inserted in center comes out clean. Cool 5 minutes in pan on rack and then turn out on rack to cool completely.

Makes one 9-inch loaf.

The islands are famous for fresh seafood, which is a perfect complement to High Tea. Here, a lovely salad of shrimp, apples, olives, scallions, avocado, and tomatoes is served in a scallop shell dish, left.

Chinese Tea: The Dim Sum Lunch

Yum cha is Chinese for the drinking of fragrant tea and eating of traditional tea lunch food. Dim sum, classical Chinese tea fare, is eaten either at a teahouse or served at home. Literally translated, dim sum means "a point on the heart"; this translation illustrates the reverence for this culinary ritual. The traditional Chinese village teahouse was a place for men to gather and discuss the local crops, news, or business transactions. The teahouse was a one-room affair, lined with windows and scattered with tables. Wealthy, elderly gentlemen would amble in, one perhaps parading a splendid nightingale or long-tailed finch in a bamboo cage. Today, in cities such as Hong Kong, two-storied restaurants serve dim sum to families celebrating occasions like the August Moon or Dragon Boat festival. However, a birthday, anniversary, cocktail party, or simply a love of the steamed bun makes a fine excuse for a Chinese tea lunch.

You will need to prepare the foods in advance because the host or hostess is always seated with the guests. Low blackwood chairs surrounding a marble-topped table would accurately reproduce the elegant teahouse setting, but any banquet-style or coffee table will do. Handpainted ibis or storks fly on folding screens, which add a touch of intimacy, or if you fancy live birds, you might have gold finches or canaries sing from gilded cages. If you will be near a window, line the ledge with open, opaque fans for diffused lighting. On the table place a shallow bowl of water with floating flower heads and greens for a lily pond effect. Set each place with beige napkins under wooden or lacquered chopsticks resting on boxlike holders. A knife and fork should be offered to those who do not enjoy chopsticks. You might also use rolled terrycloths tied with bright red ribbons for napkins. A lacquered tray in the center of the table will neatly hold small bowls of dipping sauces. Lacquered fans make interesting plates, or you might opt for the traditional blue-and-white china. Black china is bold and has great visual impact when the dump-

Courtesy of Bing & Grondahl Inc.

Combine traditional Chinese-inspired implements—rattan trays, chopsticks, and china—with Western teacups and flatware for a novel tea for two.

lings and other tea fare are centered on the dishes, or look for octagonal-shaped plates with drawings of dragons or Chinese calligraphy. These are striking additions to the table, particularly if you place them on larger, round china with gold bands. Set a large pot of fragrant green tea on the table with small, glazed pottery or porcelain glass cups at each place.

To begin the tea, bring a large bowl of boiling water to the table. Each person should dip his or her teacup in this water, and dry it on a cloth provided at each place. Then, offer warm, moist towels scented with lemon water for wiping hands. Remove the bowl and towels before pouring the tea. When ready to serve, pour the tea with the spout facing away from the guest. One guest takes the tea and offers it to a fellow diner who accepts it with both hands. The tea should be drunk in the Chinese manner, by sucking in cool air while sipping the hot liquid, a noisy but sensible way to avoid burnt lips. When the teapot is empty, a guest should signal the host by taking the teapot lid off. When one's cup is filled, thanks are said by simply rapping two fingers sharply on the table top. This way, general conversation is not interrupted. Such silent dialogue respects teahouse protocol, a language which speaks to the joys of the heart.

The food is served from a rolling cart, or can be presented on a series of prepared trays. You should present a diverse selection. Offer choices of golden-baked, crunchy-fried, or translucent-steamed dumplings filled with beancurd, shrimp and scallions, or spicy pork. Shrimp balls, tea eggs, pork ribs, potstickers, spring rolls, spicy squid, fried rice, wontons, turnip cake, egg custard, spiced nuts, almond cookies, and Chinese crullers are standard dim sum fare. Buns are an important part of the ceremony, and they can be stuffed with barbecued pork or sweets such as date filling. Recipes for these dishes are available in a number of well-written dim sum books. And, of course, in most major cities one can find a Chinese bakery. In traditional Cantonese teahouses, dim sum maidens sing songs alerting customers to the servings. They call out the names of dishes in a singsong and offer them to the customers, who respond by pointing to what looks appetizing.

John Dominus/Wheeler Pictures

Steamed dumplings, spare ribs, fried rice, and lemon custard tarts are part of the culinary variety of dim sum.

Steamed Buns Filled with Vegetables

Dough:

2 packages active dry yeast
1 1/2 tablespoons sugar
1 cup lukewarm water
1 tablespoon peanut oil
3 cups all-purpose flour, sifted

In small bowl, combine yeast and sugar with 1/3 cup of the lukewarm water. Set aside 2 to 5 minutes in warm place until mixture is bubbly and has expanded in volume. Stir in oil.

Meanwhile, place flour in warm, large mixing bowl. Make a well in center and add yeast mixture and remaining 2/3 cup water. Gather dough into soft firm ball. Turn out onto lightly floured work surface and knead 10 to 15 minutes until smooth and elastic, adding more flour as necessary. Shape into ball and place in large oiled bowl, turning to coat with oil. Cover bowl with damp towel and set aside in warm, draft-free place 45 minutes or until dough is doubled in bulk.

Punch down dough and knead again on lightly floured work surface 2 to 3 minutes. Separate dough into 2 equal portions. Shape each portion into a long cylinder about 2 inches in diameter. With sharp knife, slice each cylinder into 12 equal rounds, about 1 inch thick. Place rounds on lightly floured baking sheets at least 2 inches apart, cover with damp towel and set in warm, draft-free place to rise, approximately 45 to 55 minutes or until again doubled in bulk.

Vegetable filling:

3 tablespoons olive oil
1 1/2 cups blanched, diced turnips (1/2 pound whole turnips)

1 cup each seeded and diced green and red bell peppers (1 large one each)
1 cup diced domestic mushrooms (4 ounces whole mushrooms)
1/2 cup chopped scallions, green tops included (about 6 scallions)
2 tablespoons sesame oil
2 teaspoons soy sauce
2 tablespoons chopped fresh cilantro
1 teaspoon dry mustard
Freshly ground black pepper to taste

In large skillet, heat olive oil over low heat. Stir in turnips, peppers, mushrooms, and scallions. Stirring constantly, sprinkle in remaining ingredients. Raise heat to moderate-high and sauté 8 minutes or until vegetables are tender. Cool.

To fill buns: Working with 1 dough round at a time while keeping others covered, flatten each round with palm of hand, then roll out into flat circle, about 4 1/2 inches in diameter. Cupping dough circle in palm of one hand, place 1 heaping tablespoon filling in center. Gather edges up and around filling, twisting and pinching together tightly to seal. Place buns twisted side down on 2-inch squares of wax paper 2 inches apart in deep baking pans (2 1/2 to 3 inches deep). Cover with dry towel and set aside in warm place 30 minutes until dough is soft and springy.

In bamboo or metal steamer, add enough water to come up to within 1 inch below steamer rack. Arrange as many buns on wax paper as will fit 1 inch apart on rack in steamer. Over high heat, bring water to boil, cover pan tightly, and steam 10 to 15 minutes. Transfer buns to warm plate. Repeat procedure with remaining buns. Serve hot.

Makes 24 three-inch buns.

Shui chow, shrimp encased in steamed translucent dumplings is an appropriate dim sum food.

Fried, stuffed taro horn is filled with puru or vegetables and served in bright paper cups.

ASIAN TEA CUSTOMS

In Sri Lanka, tea is consumed all day and night, and is always offered to a visitor. In rural Sri Lanka, tea boutiques are identified by a large cluster of bananas hanging in the doorway. The tea shop is a kind of pub for the tea garden employees who stop in the village to sip a cup of tea and eat an indigenous snack called betal leaf, converse, and rest. Samovar-like urns are used for boiling water; the charcoal that fuels the furnace of these hot-pots is coconut shell. The tea is a hearty brew made from a generous amount of leaves. The liquid is strained into brass cups, and the tea is poured from one brass cup to another until it is cool enough to be poured into smaller serving cups. Tea is called the "gift of the gods."

In Burma, tea is symbolic of union, and a mixture of tea leaves soaked in oil is shared by a newlywed couple. The Burmese also enjoy a pickled tea dressed with sesame oil, toasted sesame seeds, fried garlic, powdered shrimp, monkey nuts, and roasted peas. Similarly, Tjampa is a Tibetan tea made with rice or ground beans and buttered tea.

In China, herbalists run shops that are frequented by people seeking cures for imbalanced bodies, the result of too many "hot" or "cool" factors that come from stress, overeating, or distressing news of visiting relatives. Tea is prescribed as a medicine with restorative powers.

Vietnam's tea plantations are in the cool highlands of the Central province of Dulat. A tea called Blao is named for the tea gardens. It is a mixture of dried flowers such as chyrsanthemums, roses, jasmine, and the favorite, lotus blossom. When this tea is served, it is often accompanied by poetry. Friends gathering for tea often present original poems.

American Variety

American tea is a diverse culinary affair, a melting pot of regional differences that can combine to comprise a vast and varied fare. America is also rich with folk art, which can provide a lovely theme for the teatime setting. You can draw from the spartan elegance of the Shakers, the earthy and rich hues of the Indians in the Southwest, or New England's more formal colonial designs. Whatever the theme, American tea is a setting where anything goes so long as there are boards groaning with heaping portions, and tables made festive with collected objects heralding the many heritages of the nation. This is a tea to which you will want to invite a lot of guests to sample the bountiful food.

Select a long, antique table with slatted or old painted chairs. To cover your table, think of Early American colors reflecting natural pigments such as ochre, rose, saffron, and indigo. Fabrics with small flower prints give a country look, as do stripes. You might even try a red, white, and blue theme if you feel patriotic. Amish design quilts and needlepoint cushions add quaint charm to the room. Use an earthenware jug full of sunflowers or a wooden goose decoy for a centerpiece. Handpainted stoneware crocks give festive color, and paper-covered baskets can be filled with crushed bayberry and dried rose petals to scent the air. Play Stephen Foster songs to set the mood.

Set the table with Early American pewter or handpainted plates, cups, and pitchers depicting primitive drawings. Redware pottery, made for generations by the Pennsylvania Dutch from the native clay, is particularly attractive. Other characteristic china are round or hexagonal plates with solid-colored borders and a central drawing of a clipper ship or flowers. When selecting flatware, look for pistol grips or heavy-handled silver pieces. Hand-dipped or honeycomb candles add a final touch of warmth and native spirit to the table.

The fare should include indigenous American recipes as well as recipes from the Dutch, English, and Eastern European settlers, not to mention Native American food. Hearty wheat grain breads hail from the Midwest, cornmeal sticks come from the South; wild blueberry teacakes date back to the Mayflower, and Connecticut gingerbreads moistened by butter-

Susan M. Duane

Primitive toys, the Stars and Stripes, and country-inspired tableware are appropriate to American tea.

milk, popular even today, were being baked while the revolutionary colonists hid their charter in a resplendent oak. Pumpkin cookies with lemon icing are an adaptation of the American Indian's love for the orange squash. Pecans are a quintessentially Southern, and add a delightful crunch to strawberry-pecan bread made with cornmeal. Baking powder biscuits can be served with jams made from New England's beach plums.

Early American tea fare is lavish, to say the least. Martha Washington served tea to accompany her famous "Great Cake" made with forty eggs, a few pounds of butter, and no knowledge of cholesterol. Scripture Cake has ingredients which read: Judges 5:25, Jeremiah 6:20, and Isaiah 10:14. Believe it or not, these translate to mean one cup of butter, three cups of sugar, and six eggs. Both cakes have recipes which can be found in New England heritage cookbooks. If you think they sound slightly absurd, simply serve the South's Lady Baltimore Cake which is a tall, iced, almond-flavored beauty rich with raisins, figs, and nuts. The 1930s toll house chocolate chip, an adaptation of the colonial butter drop cookie, is a

Randy O'Rourke

Iced tea, an American favorite, is a perfect accompaniment to biscuits and cookies on a summer afternoon.

TEA AT SLEEPY HOLLOW

The Dutch were the first importers of tea, and when they settled in New Amsterdam, they continued to enjoy their discovery with a host of recipes that made use of the copius fall harvests. Washington Irving's Ichabod Crane indulged in such a tea when he visited the Van Tassel mansion in Tarrytown near the banks of the Hudson River. Irving described the food-laden tables in the state parlor when he wrote that what captured Ichabod's eye was "not those of the bevy of buxom lassies, their luxurious display of red and white; but the ample charms of a genuine Dutch country tea-table, in the sumptuous time of autumn. Such heaped-up platters of cakes of various and almost indescribable kinds, known only to experienced Dutch housewives! There was the oly koek [pastry fried in deep fat], and the crisp and crumbling cruller; sweet cakes and short cakes, ginger cakes and honey cakes, and the whole family of cakes. And then there were apple pies and peach pies and pumpkin pies; besides slices of ham and smoked beef; and moreover delectable dishes of preserved plums, and peaches, and pears, and quinces; not to mention broiled shad and roasted chickens; together with bowls of milk and cream, all mingled higgledy-piggledy, pretty much as I have enumerated them, with the motherly tea-pot sending up its clouds of vapor from the midst—Heaven bless the mark!"

Sun tea—an American innovation—brews in the warming rays of the sun.

Gordon E. Smith

sure favorite. American muffins are as symbolic of the United States as the stars and stripes, or even as apple pie (which you can serve with a cheddar cheese). The American muffin is nothing like the round, flat, and holey English version. It is dome-shaped, can be quite large, and is chock full of fresh fruits and nuts. Tea muffins are generally sweet and spicy, and the Southwest offers a wonderful cheese and jalapeño pepper version. You can make a sampler of the North East's indigenous tastes by combining maple, cranberry, blueberry, and bran in a wonderfully satisfying muffin. The Pennsylvania Dutch enjoy their tea with a strudel topped with spiced-apple icing. Pile your muffins into Appalachian split wood or wisteria baskets and serve them with butter and jam. The tea to select is Ceylon breakfast or Earl Grey, which should be lightly brewed to suit American tastes. An herbal tea is also appropriate and would be in keeping with the colonial tradition begun by the women of Edenton, North Carolina who gathered at a tea party to toast their allegiance to the rebellious colonists by drinking "liberty tea."

American Iced "Sun" Tea

Americans love fads. In the early seventies, from the rocky coast of Maine to the swampy Florida Everglades, people were setting out jars of teabags to be brewed by the sun's rays. This is an especially wonderful version because of the tart and sweet citrus fruits that flavor the tea.

> *6 to 8 teaspoons black tea leaves*
> *1 quart cold water*
> *Juice of 2 lemons*
> *Juice of 1 orange*
> *Superfine sugar to taste*
> *Orange and lemon half-moon slices to garnish*

Combine tea and water in 1-quart glass jar; stir. Cap jar and set in sun 2 to 3 hours, at room temperature at least 6 hours, or in refrigerator overnight.

Add lemon and orange juices and sugar (or pass sugar separately when serving).

Stir well or shake in jar. Strain into tall glasses. Garnish with lemon and orange slices placed on edges of glasses.

Serves 4.

Pumpkin Cookies

These plump, iced cookies are reminiscent of baked goods made by Native Americans.

1/2 cup (1 stick) unsalted butter
1 cup light brown sugar
2 eggs, beaten
1 cup pumpkin puree
1 cup all-purpose flour
1 teaspoon baking soda
1 teaspoon baking powder
1/2 teaspoon salt
1/2 teaspoon ground cinnamon
1/2 teaspoon ground ginger
1/2 teaspoon ground nutmeg
1 cup whole wheat flour
Grated zest of 1 lemon
1 cup raisins
1 cup chopped walnuts or other nuts

Lemon icing:

1 cup confectioners' sugar
Grated zest of 1 lemon
2 tablespoons lemon juice, or more as needed

In large mixing bowl, cream butter. Gradually beat in sugar. Beat in eggs, one at a time, and the pumpkin. Mix well.

In separate bowl, sift together all-purpose flour, baking soda, baking powder, salt, and spices. Add to pumpkin mixture; mix well. Stir in whole wheat flour and lemon zest until well combined. Stir in raisins and nuts.

Drop by heaping tablespoons onto greased cookie sheets fairly close together but not touching. Flatten slightly with the back of a spoon. Bake in preheated oven at 350° for 12 to 15 minutes.

Meanwhile, in small mixing bowl, combine sugar, lemon zest and enough lemon juice to make desired spreading consistency of icing.

Place cookie sheets on racks to cool cookies slightly. Then while still warm, spread on icing with pastry brush. Remove cookies from cookie sheets, place on racks and cool completely.

Makes approximately 4 dozen cookies.

Chocolate chip cranberry muffins and tea loaves are standard teatime fare.

Gordon E. Smith

Maple-Cranberry/Blueberry Muffins

Muffins appear in various sizes, with ingredients ranging from sweet to savory. They are taken with breakfast, lunch, or dinner—and always appear at an American tea table.

> 1 cup all-purpose flour
> 1 cup unprocessed whole bran flakes
> 1 cup unsweetened wheat germ
> 1 teaspoon baking powder
> 1 teaspoon baking soda
> 2 eggs, beaten
> 1 1/4 cup pure maple syrup
> 1 cup buttermilk
> 2 cups cranberries or blueberries

Combine dry ingredients in medium mixing bowl. Set aside.

In large mixing bowl, beat together liquid ingredients. Add dry mixture, stirring until just incorporated. Fold in berries.

Fill 2-inch muffin tins a good 3/4 full with batter. Bake in preheated oven at 400° for 15 minutes or until cake tester inserted in center comes out clean.

Makes 18 muffins.

The toll house chocolate chip cookie is an American invention that goes well with tea.

Strawberry-Pecan Bread

This is a festive loaf that celebrates the summer fruit and the indigenous American nut. The interesting addition of cornmeal adds a flavorful hint of the Southwest.

> 2 cups all-purpose flour
> 1 cup cornmeal
> 1 1/2 teaspoons baking powder
> 1 teaspoon baking soda
> 1/2 teaspoon salt
> 1 cup sugar
> 2 eggs, beaten
> 1/4 cup (4 tablespoons) unsalted butter, melted
> 1/4 cup sour cream
> 1 teaspoon vanilla
> 2 1/2 cups chopped strawberries, crushed with
>   the back of a spoon
> 3/4 cup chopped pecans

In medium mixing bowl, sift together flour, cornmeal, baking powder, baking soda and salt. Set aside.

In large mixing bowl, beat sugar and eggs until light in color. Add butter, sour cream, and vanilla and beat well. Stir dry mixture into wet until thoroughly incorporated. Fold in strawberries and pecans.

Turn into greased 10-inch loaf pan. Bake in preheated oven at 350° for 1 hour or until cake tester inserted in center comes out clean.

Makes one 10-inch loaf.

French Five O'clock Tea

France is associated with tea both because of Marcel Proust and because of the famous light touch the French bakers have with pastries. The five o'clock tea is a Parisian version of the British four o'clock repast, and one which is based on many regional baking specialties.

To present a French tea, set an intimate bistro-type table with doily placemats or a white tablecloth. Use simple silver flatware. Pink or blue jacquard napkins are lovely with faience handpainted plates rimmed with flower buds, or with French Quimper china. For bold color, display Folies Bergère or Toulouse-Lautrec prints. If you like a softer setting, play with the pastels of Monet's water lilies by using plates which reflect the Impressionist's colors. Lalique-style glassware or a small bud vase will add elegance, and a few bright poppies can look lovely in a small blue-glass apothecary jar. You might play Josephine Baker's "Jaix Deux Amours," or Edith Piaf to evoke visions of the Eiffel Tower and the banks of the Seine.

Commercy, in Alsace-Lorraine, is the home of the venerable madeleine that sent Proust reeling into many volumes recalling his past. In *À la recherche du temps perdu* he writes that the small tea cake, shaped like the "fluted scallop of a pilgrim's shell," was offered with a cup of lime-flavored tea to cheer him on a winter's day. His recollection of dipping the madeleine into this infusion has forever linked France, and the delicate cake, with tea. Serve your madeleines piled in a large scallop shell or on a small silver tray lined with a doily. Other desserts can be wheeled in on a cart. Try longe de chat dipped in chocolate or Alsatian orange cookies, which complement the French tisanes. Nonnettes, or "little nuns," are teatime gingerbreads and are as popular as the simpler honeybread. Anise-flavored macaroons are a

Bill Rothschild

A pair of bunnies keep watch over this centerpiece of meringue cookies and marzipan.

surprising treat. A favorite at teatime is a dark chocolate cake with an apricot jam, sandwiched, and served with whipped cream. Sugar-coated almonds or glacé fruit can be placed in small silver or crystal bowls. It is quite simple to make Burgundy's black cherry clafouti, which is lovely dusted with powdered sugar, or a chestnut flour cake, both of which can be placed on a round cake stand. All these desserts can be either bought or made at home, and will surely command attention at your teatable. With them serve an herbal tea. In Grasse, where the fields are surrounded by lavender, they drink a sweet tea made from this flower. You can acquire it at a specialty store, or serve lime, orange, or chamomile teas, all of which ensure a hearty "Bon Appetit!"

Rue de France

Shown here is a tea set by a window with French-inspired curtains and colorful cookies and sweets.

Alsatian Orange Cookies

These are from a family recipe which survived the territorial squabbles of France and Germany to emerge, triumphantly, as a melt-in-the-mouth tea-time cookie.

> 2 1/2 cups all-purpose flour, sifted
> 1/4 teaspoon salt
> 1/4 teaspoon baking soda
> 1 cup vegetable shortening
> 1/2 cup granulated sugar
> 1/2 cup packed light brown sugar
> 1 medium egg, beaten
> 2 tablespoons fresh orange juice
> 1 teaspoon grated orange zest

In medium mixing bowl, sift flour again with salt and baking soda.

In separate, large mixing bowl, cream shortening with sugars. Mix in egg, orange juice, and orange zest and beat thoroughly.

Add flour mixture gradually, mixing well after each addition.

Drop by tablespoons, 2 1/2 inches apart, onto ungreased cookie sheets. Bake in preheated oven at 400° for 12 minutes until golden.

Makes approximately 30 cookies.

DEJA VU

I raised to my lips a spoonful of the tea in which I had soaked a morsel of the cake. No sooner had the warm liquid, and the crumbs with it, touched my palate than a shudder ran through my whole body, and I stopped, intent upon the extraordinary changes that were taking place. An exquisite pleasure had invaded my senses, but individual, detached, with no suggestion of its origin. And at once the vicissitudes of life had become indifferent to me, its disasters innocuous, its brevity illusory— This new sensation having had on me the effect which love has of filling me with a precious essence; or rather this essence was not in me, it was myself. I had ceased to feel mediocre, accidental, mortal. Whence could it have come to me, this all powerful joy? I was conscious that it was connected with the taste of tea and cake, but that it infinitely transcended those savours, could not, indeed, be of the same nature as theirs. Whence did it come? What did it signify? How could I seize upon and define it?

—Marcel Proust, *Remembrance of Things Past*

Courtesy of Le Jacquard Francais

French jacquard linens and molded glass accessories will set the mood for your Parisian tea.

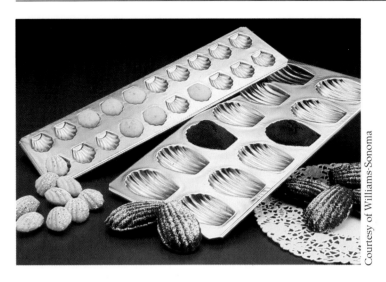

Scallop shell madeleines are lightly dusted with confectioners' sugar.

Courtesy of Williams-Sonoma

Cocoa Madeleines

Feathery light, with a hint of rich chocolate, made for dipping in fragrant teas.

> *3 eggs, room temperature*
> *3/4 cup sugar*
> *1 tablespoon Cointreau or other orange-flavored*
>   *liqueur*
> *1 cup sifted all-purpose flour*
> *1/2 cup unsweetened cocoa*
> *3/4 clarified unsalted butter*

In large bowl, beat eggs with sugar until thick and lightly colored. Beat in Cointreau.

Sift together flour and cocoa. Gently fold into egg and sugar mixture.

Fold 1/2 cup of the clarified butter into batter until barely incorporated. Tightly cover bowl with plastic wrap and refrigerate a few hours, or overnight, until completely chilled.

With pastry brush, grease 2 madeleine pans (of 12 madeleine molds each) with some of the remaining clarified butter. Turn pans upside down on wax paper to allow excess butter to drip off so it does not pool in each cake mold. Refrigerate the pans 10 minutes; repeat process, making sure butter is chilled and set in molds at each coating.

Spoon rounded tablespoons of batter into each mold. If batter is very cold, gently press spoonful of batter in center to spread it slightly into mold. Bake in center of preheated oven at 425° for 5 minutes. Reduce heat to 375° and bake 8 minutes more until just crisping at edges.

Remove from oven and tap pans sharply against a flat surface to loosen madeleines. Turn out cakes onto racks to cool slightly. Serve warm.

Makes 24 madeleines.

African Farm Tea

If you have a porch, this is the perfect place to set your African tea. Use white wicker chairs with matching side tables or canvas sling-back chairs with faux bamboo or wooden side tables. Tall clay vessels can display peacock feathers, upside-down pith helmets can be unexpectedly filled with hydrangeas, and budding succulents can represent the low, thick thorn trees of the bush. Hide a sculpture of an unblinking giraffe behind a sheath of dried grasses. Blend natural field colors of light green, red, sparks of yellow, or the crimson of the flowering flame trees, with the bush hues of dried brown grasses or verdant jungle greens. Play with fabrics sporting animal motifs and colors such as zebra stripes, leopard spots, the golden brown manes of lions, the pulsating pink of flamingoes, the scalelike geometric patterns of snakes, or the plumelike feathers of ostriches.

Mix wooden bowls with English stoneware, and if you can, use onyx- or ivory-color handled flatware. The silver should be smooth and polished like a gleaming lake in the grasslands. Use bongo drums as cake stands, and string colorful handpainted beads around plates of sandwiches or cookies.

The food you serve should be largely influenced by the British taste in afternoon tea. But, there are some unusual dishes worth investigating in African cookbooks. Pineapple fritters are soaked in local rum and served with a thick cream made from eggs and boiled milk. The pineapple is dipped into the cream and broiled, then fried in oil. The deep brown and crunchy fruit is finally sprinkled with sugar and cinnamon. It is a treat alive with rich spices. (You can substitute bananas for the pineapple.) Another dish is baked yam, which is mashed and rolled into naturally sweet balls called fru-frus. From South Africa there are Dutch influenced tea sweets which are distinctive and delicious. Grape bunlet, known as *mosbolletje*, is made from fermented grape juice, which causes the dough to rise. Many South African

Ken Druse

children can recall how the dark brown bread, pulled from the oven, perfumes the entire house from parlor to gabled attic. It is eaten with a Quince or mulberry jam. Other popular tea fare includes almond topped soetkoekies rich with spices, and krakelinge, which are crisp, pretzel-like cookies dusted with sugar and topped with nuts. Koesisters are famous cruller-like pastries dipped in a lemon-lime sugar glaze. Serve Kenya tea with milk, or a Ceylon black.

Judd Pilossof

Custard-based spice pies are a specialty of African farm teas, above.

Farm teas are best set outside as in this charming pagoda, left.

TEA ON THE FARM

Afternoon teas in Africa are as expected a meal as breakfast, lunch, and dinner. The farms, often spread a minimum of ten miles apart, depend on teatime for people to gather and take a moment to socialize. At four o'clock the children are called in, the workers put their equipment to rest, and families gather on wraparound verandahs of corrugated tin-roof houses for afternoon tea.

Comfortable wicker chairs and an occasional creaking swing look out on hedges with flowering succulants, roses, and hydrangeas. From the radio a soft-spoken, clipped voice reads the weather forecast. Proper gossip is shared about the neighboring farms or the price of beef. Children wield cricket bats, kick balls, swing, or play clapping games. The grandparents beckon them for a drink of iced tea or lemonade, and they pause to pat a dog sleeping in the shade. Slithering lizards crawl up the sides of the house. A cat chases a puff adder in the garden, a flower snaps, and a dog raises one eye to see if all is calm before dozing again. It is an atmosphere of regulated, calm indulgence with a meal that bears the influence of British, Malaysian, Scottish, and Dutch cuisine.

The native Somali women took a different view of the teatime habit, as Isak Dinesen described in *Out of Africa*. "As tea was served, it came out that it was only the married sister and the children who could partake of it, to the young girls it was forbidden as too exciting. They had to content themselves with cakes and did so demurely, with a good grace. There was some discussion about the little girl, who was with us,—could she still drink tea, or had she reached an age to which it would prove too dangerous? The married sister held that she might have it, but the child gave us a deep, dark, proud glance, and rejected the cup."

Lemon 'N Lime Glazed Crullers

Citrus Syrup:

4 cups sugar
3 cinnamon sticks, approximately 2 inches long
2 tablespoons each fresh lime and lemon juice
2 pieces each lime and lemon peel (3-by-1-inch)
Pinch of salt
1/4 teaspoon cream of tartar in 2 teaspoons cold
*   water*

In 2-to-3-quart saucepan, combine 2 cups water with everything but the cream of tartar mixture. Cook over moderate heat, stirring constantly until sugar dissolves. Stir in cream of tartar mixture, increase heat to high and cook covered, without stirring, until syrup reaches 230° on a candy thermometer or a small amount dropped into ice water instantly forms a coarse thread.

Remove pan from heat immediately and place in large bowl of ice water. Stir gently until syrup cools to room temperature. Remove and discard cinnamon sticks and lemon/lime peels. Refrigerate syrup at least 2 hours or until thoroughly chilled.

Crullers:

4 cups all-purpose flour
4 teaspoons baking powder
1/2 teaspoon ground cinnamon
1/2 teaspoon ground nutmeg
1/2 teaspoon salt
2 tablespoons each cold butter and shortening or
*   lard, cut into small pieces*
1 1/2 cups buttermilk
Vegetable oil for frying

In large mixing bowl, sift together flour, baking powder, cinnamon, nutmeg, and salt. With pastry blender or two knives, cut in butter and shortening until mixture resembles coarse meal. Slowly pour in buttermilk in thin stream while constantly stirring with wooden spoon until all ingredients are well-combined. Knead mixture until it forms soft, pliable dough. Divide dough equally into three balls and cover loosely with dampened dish towel.

Working with one ball of dough at a time, turn out onto lightly floured work surface. Pat into 1-inch-thick rectangle, then roll into rectangle approximately 12-inches long by 6-inches wide and 1/4-inch thick. Even off edges with pastry wheel or sharp knife. Cut rectangle crosswise into four 3-inch-wide strips and then divide and cut each of these lengthwise into three 1-inch-wide strips. Cut evenly lengthwise across the center of the big rectangle to make a total of 24 rectangles, each 3 by 1 inch. Braid into crullers as follows: Starting from the narrow bottom end of each rectangle, cut lengthwise into three equal strips to within about 1/2 inch of top edge. Interweave the strips into a tight braid and pinch the loose bottom ends together and set crullers aside on wax paper and cover with dampened kitchen towel. Roll, cut, and shape remaining balls of dough.

Pour vegetable oil into deep fryer or large heavy saucepan to depth of 2 or 3 inches. Heat until oil reaches 375° on deep-fat frying thermometer. Fry crullers 4 or 5 at a time, turning them with slotted spoon, 4 minutes or until they are dark golden brown and crisp. Drain briefly on paper towels.

While still hot, immerse crullers in cold citrus syrup for approximately 1 minute with tongs. Transfer to wire rack set over paper towels to drain completely. Serve warm or at room temperature.

Makes 6 dozen crullers.

Gordon E. Smith

Another version of koesisters, these are larger crullers drizzled with a white sugar icing.

▚▞▚▞▚▞▚▞ DESERT TEA ▚▞▚▞▚▞▚▞

In Northwestern Africa, harsh life on the Sahara is relieved by the refreshing ritual of drinking tea. During wars, nomadic traveling, or any desert adventure, all activity stops many times a day for tea. Everyone is required to drink three glasses when a pot of the sugary mint tea is made. There is a saying that accompanies the taking of tea, and it provides insight into the essence of life lived under a glaring sun where sometimes one's only company is one's shadow on the sand. It is said that the first cup of tea is as bitter as life; the second as sweet as love; the third as gentle as death.

Moroccan Mint

The ancient rites of cuisine are observed by the people of North Africa's Morocco where Allah rules over the ceremonial tea taken at home. To present a Moroccan tea, you can improvise and still follow the ritual. It is a complete meal, quite filling, and a lot of fun because of the exotic environment.

You will need a low coffee table or platform surrounded by large, colorful pillows. Handwoven wall hangings with geometric patterns can cover the table, clashing to the point of fashionable discord with the colors and designs of the cushions. Napkins can be Indian cotton or paisley prints. In traditional homes, bright mosaics decorate the walls, their colors harmonizing with richly woven carpets. You can buy a few spectacular tiles and hang them on the walls or use them for hot plates. Terracotta or stoneware

Bill De Neergaard

dinner plates and small handleless teacups are appropriate. If you can, try to find a brass or copper teapot with a long spout.

Seat your guests on low chairs or the pillows around the table. Set each place with a plate, knife and fork (though traditionally one eats with one's fingers), a teacup, and a small finger bowl. Pass around a large pitcher of warm, lemon-scented water. The water should be poured into each finger bowl, and each person should dip three fingers in the water before drying his or her hands on the provided towels. Remove the towels and bowls on a copper tray. You are ready to begin the meal.

The traditional bstilla or pigeon pie, a sugar filo pastry dish full of plump, sweet pigeon or chicken, should start the ceremony. Next you might present a platter of chicken with prunes and honey, followed by couscous heaped into a large clay bowl. The meal ends with fekkus, slightly sweet cookies, or with a semolina dessert similar to rice pudding. Then, present the mint tea. This is made from a gunpowder green tea with sprigs of fresh mint and a lot of sugar.

If you prefer to serve a sweets only North African tea, you can find a lively array of popular teatime pastries in a Near Eastern bakery. You might look for the rich, honey-soaked baklava, cigar-shaped pastries called ''Brides Fingers,'' almond crescents made with rose water, or sponge doughnuts called Sfinges. You can also make pancakes fried in butter and top them with honey or stuff them with almonds. Again, mint tea traditionally accompanies this food.

The spice stand is a colorful—and necessary—part of the Moroccan market scene. Though you may not buy your spices in a shop like this one, you should be sure to have plenty of paprika, saffron, ginger, coriander, cardamom, caraway seeds, and cumin on hand to prepare Morocco's spicy dishes.

Mint Tea

Best taken in small, three-inch glasses. A syrupy, sweet tea made unique by the addition of pine nuts, which add a surprising crunch to the final sips.

> *3 teaspoons Gunpowder tea leaves*
> *3 tablespoons chopped fresh mint plus whole*
>   *leaves to garnish*
> *2 tablespoons sugar or to taste*
> *2 tablespoons toasted pine nuts*

Bring 4 cups water to boil. Pour into teapot over tea leaves. Add mint, sugar, and 1 tablespoon pine nuts.

Let steep 4 to 5 minutes. Stir, allow to settle, and pour tea into 4 small glasses or cups. Divide remaining pine nuts among glasses and sprinkle on top. Garnish with mint leaves.

Serves 4.

Sesame donuts are found in many Near Eastern bakeries and are dipped in sweet honey sauce.

John Dominus/Wheeler Pictures

Bill De Neergaard

Tea vendors, with their portable tea urns, are a common sight in Morocco, left.

Moroccan Aniseed Cookies

Also known as fekkus in Moroccan bakeries, the exotic spices of the Middle East flavor this light dessert.

1 package active dry yeast
1/4 cup lukewarm water, plus additional
3 to 3 1/4 cups pastry flour
1/4 teaspoon salt
1 1/4 cups confectioners' sugar plus more for
    dusting
1/2 cup (1 stick) unsalted butter, melted and
    cooled
1 scant tablespoon aniseed
1 scant tablespoon sesame seeds
1/4 cup orange flower water

In small bowl, dissolve yeast in 1/4 cup lukewarm water and set aside in warm spot until bubbly.

Meanwhile, in large mixing bowl, combine flour, salt, and sugar.

Stir in bubbling yeast, butter, aniseed, and sesame seeds.

Stir in orange flower water and then enough lukewarm water to form a firm dough, kneading until smooth.

Turn out onto work surface lightly dusted with more confectioners' sugar and divide into 4 equal portions. Roll each portion into a ball and cover with a cloth.

Working with one ball of dough at a time, shape dough into a 1-inch-thick cylinder by rolling firmly back and forth with palms and stretching the dough out to the ends to lengthen it. (NOTE: Dough will be sticky at first but will start to become manageable after some forceful rolling.) Roll dough out to 10-to-12-inch cylinder of even thickness. Repeat with remaining balls. Place on baking sheets, cover with clean dish towel and let rise in warm place 1 hour or until doubled in bulk. Prick each cylinder with a fork to deflate.

Bake in preheated oven at 375° for 20 minutes or until barely golden. (NOTE: The dough should not be cooked through.) Cool on racks overnight.

The following day, slice cylinders crosswise into very thin cookies, about 1/4-inch thick. Bake on ungreased cookie sheets in preheated oven at 350° for 10 to 15 minutes or until golden brown and dry.

Makes approximately 8 dozen cookies.

Russian Evening Tea

Russians adore formal customs, and one is always hospitable to a guest. The Russian word for hospitality translates to mean bread and salt, and it is a clearly understood decree that where there is food there shall be tea. In fact, Russians love tea and drink it all day long. Because it is customary to eat only one main meal during the day, a glass or cup of tea is perfect refreshment before or after the meal. The drink is savored as something fortifying, particularly because it is taken with a spoonful of jam or a piece of sugar. When it is combined with teatime food, as in the Evening Tea, it is a classic samovar affair that rivals the most splendid Victorian or high tea.

The center of attention is the gleaming silver or brass samovar. If you don't have access to one, use a hot water urn. Cover a large round table with a deep red paisley print or a few large, embroidered and fringed shawls. Tall brass candlesticks cascading in size, each with a slender white candle, will draw the eye to the table's center. When the wicks are lit, the flames are reflected as sparkling lights in the metal of the samovar. Handpainted Ukranian batik eggs make delightful tea table ornaments, and they can be clustered or hidden among the food. A balalaika or dulcimer serves as a charming decoration as well as a conversation piece. The flatware should be shiny, scrolled silver. Elegant porcelain tea sets are laid out for the women, and glass cups inserted in filigreed silver holders are reserved for the men. Children traditionally drink tea by pouring it from their cups to their saucers and sipping it from the dishes to

prevent burning their mouths. A china drip bowl should be set under the spigot of the samovar. You can display a carved, antique brass tea caddy full of loose tea on the table. Sugar cubes are best piled in glass bowls with pincers, and brightly colored sweet

Smithsonian Institute

The gleaming samovar has added grace to the tea table since its invention in the early eighteenth century.

jams like the garnet-red morello cherry or golden peach preserves will glisten in cut glass pots.

To begin, offer tea to your guests with the choice of a spoonful of preserves or a cube of sugar. The jam can be spooned directly into the tea, or eaten right from the dish with intermittent sips of tea. It flavors the drink and gives a boost of tart sweetness to the strong infusion. The sugar cube is traditionally clamped between the teeth while drinking the tea.

The food should be well displayed on the table. Use huge platters offering sliced meats, sausages, smoked salmon, and chicken. On smaller, round trays you can present piroshki. These turnovers are made of yeast, short, or puff pastry and filled with cottage cheese, carrot and onion, kasha, or cabbage. They can also be made bursting with sweet cheese and fruit fillings, and dusted with confectioners' sugar.

Pile breads in baskets and on wooden boards. Black breads can be sliced and topped with chopped liver or whitefish spreads. Serve a krendel, a pretzel-shaped or braided yeast bread made sweet with candied orange peel and raisins. Russian tea buns spiced with cardamom and vanilla, or tall babas, which are sweetbreads likened to the look of a chef's hat, are traditional favorites. With the breads, serve sweet pot cheese or wheels of hard cheese.

Offer a selection of cookies such as rum balls, walnut crescents, almond rings, and delicate meringues. Next to them place circular lemon or apple cakes with chocolate glaze, apricot or cranberry tarts, and tall chocolate cakes or poppy seed tortes on prominent stands. Candied orange and grapefruit peels coated in sugar will shimmer in dark, ceramic dishes. Finally, fill a basket with red pomegranates, plump purple plums, smooth golden-green pears, and sunny apricots. For this elaborate meal, serve a strong China black, India blend, or Russian Caravan tea to complement the food.

Poppy Seed Torte

A light, flourless teatime cake that combines the Slavic love of poppy seeds and hazelnuts.

1 cup poppy seeds
1 small can (5 ounces) evaporated milk
2 cups ground hazelnuts
2 tablespoons fine bread crumbs
1/2 teaspoon ground coriander
6 eggs, separated
1 cup sugar
1/2 teaspoon cream of tartar
1/8 teaspoon salt
1/2 teaspoon vanilla extract

In small bowl, soak poppy seeds in evaporated milk at least two hours at room temperature or refrigerated overnight.

In medium bowl, lightly toss together nuts, bread crumbs, and coriander and set aside.

In large mixing bowl, beat egg yolks vigorously until pale yellow and thick. Add sugar gradually, continuing to beat well, until mixture is very creamy.

In separate bowl, beat together egg whites, cream of tartar and salt until stiff but not dry.

Stir poppy seed mixture and vanilla into yolk and sugar mixture. Fold 1/4 beaten whites into this mixture. Add remaining whites and fold in. Sprinkle 1/4 of the nut mixture at a time into batter, partially folding in, until all of nut mixture has been added, then fold in completely.

Spread batter evenly in greased and floured 10-inch springform pan and bake in preheated oven at 325° for 55 minutes or until cake tester inserted in center comes out clean. Cool in pan completely before removing outer ring. Dust the top of cake with confectioners' sugar before serving.

Makes 16 slices.

Sweet Prune and Cheese Piroshki

These cream cheese dough turnovers combine the Russian adoration for dried fruits with the quintessential samovar snack. There are entire piroshki tea meals designed around these pockets of dough stuffed with sweet or savory fillings like raisins, potatoes, cabbage, or meat. This recipe will satisfy sweet tooths.

Dough:

1 eight-ounce package cream cheese, softened
1/2 cup (1 stick) unsalted butter, softened
1 1/2 cups all-purpose flour
1/4 teaspoon salt

In large mixing bowl or electric mixer, cream together cream cheese and butter thoroughly. Sift in flour and salt and work in with fingers or pastry blender until smooth. Wrap dough in plastic wrap and refrigerate at least 3 hours and up to 12.

Filling:

1 cup pitted prunes, dried apricots or
*   combination (about 4 ounces), chopped*
1/4 cup Grand Marnier or plum brandy
1 stick cinnamon (about 3 inches)
1 tablespoon grated lemon zest
1/2 teaspoon whole cloves, tied in cheesecloth
1 egg separated (white, lightly beaten)
3 to 4 tablespoons sugar, to taste
1 tablespoon unsalted butter, softened
1 tablespoon instant-blending or all-purpose
*   flour*

1/2 pound prepared farmer's cheese (To prepare
*   cheese: Press cheese through sieve and grind in*
*   meat grinder or food processor)*
1/4 teaspoon salt

Place prunes in medium saucepan and pour Grand Marnier and 1/2 cup water on top. Stir in cinnamon, lemon zest, and cloves. Cover and stew fruit over low heat about 10 minutes, stirring occasionally and adding water if liquid evaporates too quickly, or until fairly mushy. Remove to bowl to cool; discard cinnamon and cloves.

In electric mixer or food processor, combine egg yolk, sugar, and butter and beat 2 to 3 minutes. Add flour and beat 2 more minutes. Add cheese and salt and continue beating 3 more minutes or until completely blended and very smooth.

Stir in prune mixture well to combine.

Remove dough from refrigerator, turn out onto lightly floured work surface and roll out into large circle (about 20 inches in diameter and 1/8 inch thick). Cut into rounds with 3-inch cookie cutter. Gently re-roll dough scraps and cut out rounds.

Place 1 well-rounded teaspoon filling on each round, moisten edge with water, and carefully fold dough over filling so as not to lose any filling, making half-moon crescents. Press edges together and crimp with tines of a fork. Brush tops with beaten egg white; prick with fork. Place on ungreased baking sheets and bake in preheated oven at 450° for 15 to 20 minutes or until golden brown. Cool slightly, then sift confectioner's sugar on top.

Makes approximately 30 three-inch piroshki.

Gordon E. Smith

Coffee cakes are as popular as the famous tall-standing bobka, a popular Russian yeast cake that is sweet.

LONG LIVE THE SAMOVAR

The monumental Russian tribute to tea is the mighty samovar. Because the samovar is a luxury not every Russian can afford, those who are fortunate enough to own one display it with great pride. It is an object of beauty, gleaming in candlelight, that bestows gracious heat. The samovar is an adaptation of the thirteenth century Mongolian hot pot, and the name means "self-cooker." It is an urn with a wide funnel in the center where hot charcoal fires the water. In the summer the samovar is heated out of doors to avoid filling the house with smoke. In the winter a pipe extends from the samovar into the chimney. Once the water is boiled in the samovar, the entire urn is brought out to the dining area where the tea concentrate is brewed in a small, round teapot. The teapot is perched on top of the samovar where it stays warm. After the tea is brewed, it is traditional to pour the concentrate into delicate porcelain cups or glasses. Water from the samovar is used to dilute the brew.

Indian Tea

The Indian tea table is alive with colors, brass, flowers, and spicy foods that scent the air. While the custom of tea in India is a remnant of the British colonial empire, the taste for tea and its accompanying food is distinctively Indian.

Drape silk fabrics embroidered with gold thread around the room and from the ceiling for a tent effect. Use colors reflecting the spices and sounds of a busy market: throbbing pinks, mustardy ochers, yellow saffrons, cinnabar reds, rich ambers, brilliant orange, frondlike greens, and peacock blues. The colors should look as if they might be too hot to touch. You can cover the table with embroidered or batik sari material, or an Indian cotton bedspread. Something resembling the Bengal Tiger's stripes will give your table an appropriately bold look. Scatter fresh flower petals on the table top for additional color and festivity, or make a garland of flower blossoms for a centerpiece. Fill a rattan basket with lemons, limes, and ripe yellow-red mangos. Oranges can be studded with whole cloves, and long cinnamon sticks can be crossed in geometric patterns. Stuffed, painted, and mirrored elephants or brass bells make good decorations. On the walls you might hang prints of Islamic miniature paintings or photos of the Indian palaces and temples. Dhurrie rugs can cover the floor. Play Indian sitar or flute music to provide just the right atmosphere.

A mixture of large brass trays with small glass cups for tea and a brass or glass pot will lend an authentic air to your table. Stack stoneware plates, which you will fill with tea snacks and hand to guests. Painted wooden bracelets or gold, brass, and ivory bangles make wonderful napkin rings for batik cotton linens. You will not need silverware, but have finger bowls, with sliced lemons floating in the water, for cleansing the hands after eating. Use low candles in colorful holders, and place them on marble squares inlaid with rose quartz, or on covered wooden trivets.

Dan Eifert

When you are ready to serve the food, turn to each guest and touching the tips of your fingers together, form a pyramid shape with your hands. This gesture is a greeting of benediction and will signal the beginning of the festivities. The Rasgullas, fine-grained cheese formed into white balls and floating in a sticky-sweet syrup, can be presented in a cut glass or ceramic bowl. Use a slotted spoon to serve them because you don't want to eat the syrup. Place one on each plate and encourage guests to help themselves to the other tea snacks. Banana Pooris is an impressive, sweet puffed-bread sprinkled with confectioners' sugar. Spiced green plantain wafers, wheat cookies made with peppercorns, diamond-shaped deep fried cookies spiced with aromatic cardamom, and sweet turnovers filled with semolina, raisins, and pistachios, can be passed on a platter. Small bowls can be filled with cashew bunfi, a ground cashew candy served with tea.

Steamed breads and cakes made of yogurt and cream of wheat are popular teatime fare. Some are deep fried or cooked on the griddle before being stuffed with hot chili, ginger, ground cumin, and white radish. Black-eyed pea pancakes are taken with chutney relish. (A good Indian cookbook will show you how to prepare these dishes.) You might try improvising with a buckwheat pancake served with mango chutney. Deep fried vegetable pastries, available in Indian shops, are complementary to coriander-mint chutney. Be sure to include the famous samosas, deep fried, spicy potato turnovers sold by tea vendors and made at home. Any Indian tea will do, as will a fragrant spiced tea made with cloves, cinnamon, cardamom, ginger, and sweetened with honey.

Tea that is reminiscent of India is evoked with brightly colored materials, hand-carved chairs, leafy plants, and an impressive print of a tropical port.

Samosas

Indians adore snacks, and somosas are traditionally sold by outdoor tea vendors. These potato-filled turnovers are also wonderful appetizers or hors d'oeuvres.

Dough:

3 cups flour
1 teaspoon salt
3 to 4 tablespoons cold unsalted butter
3/4 cup cold water

In large mixing bowl, sift together flour and salt. With pastry blender, two knives, or your fingertips, cut or rub butter into flour until mixture resembles coarse meal. Add up to 3/4 cup cold water, one tablespoon at a time, stopping when dough begins to gather into ball. On lightly floured work surface, knead together vigorously, approximately 10 minutes, until dough is very soft and pliable. Gather dough into ball and place in oiled bowl, turning to coat with oil. Cover bowl with damp towel and set aside at least 30 minutes and up to 2 hours.

Filling:

1/4 cup vegetable oil
1 teaspoon black mustard seeds (see note)
3/4 cup peeled, minced onion (1 medium onion)
1 tablespoon peeled and grated fresh ginger root (about 1 ounce ginger)
1 fresh, hot green chile, seeded and minced
1/2 cup shelled fresh peas (about 1/2 pound in shell), or substitute frozen peas, defrosted
1/3 cup peeled and very finely diced carrot (1 medium carrot)
2 tablespoons lemon juice

(continues)

1 teaspoon garam masala (see note)
1 teaspoon anardana (see note)
1/2 teaspoon fennel seeds
1/2 teaspoon cumin seeds
1/2 teaspoon ground coriander
1/4 teaspoon cayenne pepper
1/4 teaspoon turmeric
4 cups scrubbed, boiled, 1/4-inch diced potatoes
   (2 medium 1/2-pound potatoes)
Approximately 2 1/2 quarts vegetable oil for
   deep-fat frying
(NOTE: Black mustard seeds, garam masala, and
   anardana are available at Indian food shops
   or other specialty food stores, see appendix.)

In large, 10- to 12-inch skillet, heat vegetable oil over moderate heat. Add mustard seeds, stirring occasionally, until they begin to crackle, about 2 to 3 minutes. Add onion and ginger. Stirring very frequently, fry until onion is soft and golden brown, 3 to 4 minutes. Add chile, then peas, carrots, and 3 tablespoons water. (NOTE: If using frozen peas, add later—see below.) Cover, reduce heat to low and simmer until peas and carrots are just crisp tender, about 2 minutes. Stir occasionally and add additional water if skillet dries out. Add remaining ingredients—including frozen peas, if using—and stir to blend. Continue cooking gently on low, stirring frequently, 3 to 4 minutes. Transfer mixture to bowl to cool to room temperature.

Fill samosas: Turn dough out onto lightly floured work surface; knead lightly. Divide dough into 24 equal balls, about 1 1/2 inches in diameter. Keep remaining balls covered with damp towel while working with one at a time. Flatten dough ball and roll out into circle about 6 inches in diameter. With pastry wheel or sharp knife, cut circle in half. Pick up one half, moisten straight edge with finger dipped in water and form a cone, sealing moistened overlapping edge. Fill cone with approximately 1 tablespoon potato filling and moisten and press top edges closed, overlapping one edge over the other and crimping with fingers or tines of fork. Place on platter in cool spot. Continue with remaining dough balls. (NOTE: Samosas may be made up to 3 hours ahead of time, refrigerated in airtight containers or covered with plastic wrap.)

Fry samosas: Into large pot, wok or deep-fat fryer, pour 2 to 3 inches vegetable oil and heat over moderate-low until oil reaches temperature of 375° on deep-fat frying thermometer. Drop in as many samosas as will lie in single layer. Fry slowly at 375° until golden brown on all sides, 2 to 3 minutes, turning them over as each side gets done. Transfer to platter or baking dish lined with paper towels and keep warm in oven while continuing with remaining samosas. Serve warm or room temperature with coriander-mint or other chutney, passed separately.

Makes 48 two-and-a-half-inch samosas.

Peter Menzel/Wheeler Pictures

Bright turbans adorn the tea sellers who set up shop on every corner in India.

TEA AT DAWN

Tea in India is brewed at the crack of dawn. In hot weather people often sleep in courtyards under softly draped mosquito netting. They wake to the murmured chants of hymns echoing from a room reserved for prayers. By six A.M. the family is gathered to join in drinking a sweet, milky tea with a piece of fruit. In the winter, tea is often taken in front of the samovar, which exudes a welcome warmth to bodies still chilled by the morning air.

In rural India, tea is brewed in a *dekchi*, a pan held over an open fire. As the sun rises, water is boiled in this pan before the leaves are added, and a lid is placed tightly over the *dekchi* for a few minutes of brewing. The tea liquor is removed by a brass ladle and portioned into *khulahs*, unglazed clay bowls. The first sip of tea is often the first event in a new day.

The tea ritual and the elaborate Indian railroad system are intertwined in the legacy of the British Empire. It is a mode of travel dependent on tea to fuel the passengers. Breakfast is served to first class travelers on the sleeper trains by turbaned waiters who precariously perch themselves outside moving cars as they pass trays loaded with cups and saucers. The train travels past bazaars where merchants sell rubies, rugs, and rifles as weather-worn faces gather around samovars to exchange stories and goods. Sometimes the train will stop in the early morning in the middle of nowhere. For no apparant reason it will sit for hours. At this time, children will mysteriously appear beside the railcars and sell tea in small clay cups.

Indian Cheese in Sweet Fragrant Syrup

Cheese:

2 quarts milk
Approximately 1/4 cup lemon juice

In large, heavy saucepan, bring milk to boil. Reduce heat to low and slowly stir in 1/4 cup lemon juice, stirring constantly with wooden spoon until milk curdles (solid curds separating from thin, watery whey). Remove from heat immediately, cover and set aside 10 minutes. (NOTE: Add lemon juice slowly; if the curd forms before all the juice has been added, do not add it all as this will only harden the curd. Conversely, if the curd has only partially formed and the whey remains milky, add a little more juice until separation occurs.)

Strain off whey through 2 to 3 layers of cheesecloth placed in colander or sieve. Rinse curd gently under cold tap water. Bring up 4 corners of cheesecloth and tie together. Gently squeeze bundle to extract excess water. Suspend bundle to drain 1 1/2 to 2 hours (a good spot is the kitchen faucet).

Turn cheese out onto clean, smooth work surface (such as marble or formica). Knead with palm and heel of hand, spreading it out, gathering it up, and repeating process until it becomes cohesive and of a very fine, slightly grainy, spongy consistency, about 10 to 15 minutes. Form into ball and set aside.

Syrup:

4 cups sugar
10 whole cardamom pods (see note)
1 teaspoon fine-grained semolina or farina
3 to 4 drops rose essence (see note)
10 blanched almonds, cut in half and toasted
(NOTE: *Cardamom pods and rose essence are available in Indian food shops or other specialty food stores.*)

In large skillet, put 2 cups sugar, 5 cardamom pods and 6 cups water. Simmer over moderate heat, stirring occasionally until sugar has completely dissolved, 4 to 5 minutes. Turn heat to low and simmer gently 2 minutes. Remove from heat and set aside. (This is the first—or thin—syrup.)

For a second (heavy) syrup: In medium saucepan, combine remaining 2 cups sugar and 5 cardamom pods with 3 1/2 cups water. Bring to fast simmer over moderate heat until sugar has dissolved; reduce heat to low and simmer 2 minutes. Remove from heat; pour into serving bowl (leave in cardamom pods).

Make balls: Flatten out cheese ball, sprinkle semolina and rose essence on top and mix in and knead thoroughly. Divide cheese evenly and form into 20 balls (about 1-inch in diameter), compressing cheese slightly. Press almond half into center of each ball and re-form.

Bring first syrup to simmer over moderate heat. Drop in cheese balls, bring to simmer again and cook gently 5 minutes, rotating balls very gently with spoon. Turn up heat to rapid simmer (but do not boil), sprinkle balls with 2 tablespoons water, cover and cook 10 minutes. The balls should swell up slightly. Uncover, sprinkle on another 2 tablespoons water, cover and cook another 10 minutes. Remove from heat. Transfer cheese balls with slotted spoon to bowl of heavy syrup. Cover and refrigerate at least 4 and up to 24 hours. Using slotted spoon, serve 2 to 3 cheese balls per person, room temperature or cold.

Makes 20 cheese balls.

Courtesy of Tea Board of India

Samosas are standard cuisine in India. Sold by vendors on every street corner, these fried pastries are usually filled with potatoes and peas, but you can substitute just about anything.

Hot Spiced Tea Punch

Redolent with the flavors of India combined with the European taste for mulled ciders and wines, this spiced drink is both refreshing and relaxing.

12 whole cardamom pods, or substitute whole
  allspice
1/2 teaspoon whole cloves
1 stick cinnamon (about 2 inches)
4 tablespoons Darjeeling tea leaves
1 bottle (750 ml.) hearty Burgundy
1/4 cup honey
Cinnamon sticks to garnish

In large saucepan, bring 1 quart plus 1 cup water and spices to boil. Remove from heat, add tea, and stir. Cover and steep 5 minutes. Strain tea and return to saucepan.

Over low heat, add wine and honey and warm gently, stirring occasionally, about 5 to 10 minutes (be careful not to boil). Pour into punch bowl or ladle into mugs; garnish with cinnamon sticks.

Makes 2 quarts.

Japanese Way of Tea

The great sixteenth-century tea master, Sen Rikyu, was questioned about the nature of tea. He answered, "Tea is not difficult. [It] suggests the coolness in summer and warmth in winter. Set the charcoal so that the water will boil. The flowers should be arranged as if they were still in the field." To those words the questioner exclaimed, "Anyone can do that." Sen Rikyu replied, "If that is so, then I will become your student and you will become my teacher."

This humbling dialogue about *Chado*, the Japanese "way of tea," hints at the spiritual importance of the ceremony that takes many years and a lot of patience to learn. Chado is one of the cornerstones of Japanese culture. It trains people to attain enlightenment and reflects tranquility and a calm mind. Books, tea paraphernalia, and utensils are crafted by skilled artisans to be used only in this ritual. Very specific rules of etiquette are followed. Sen Rikyu believed the four principles of tea—harmony, purity, respect, and tranquility—should be maintained throughout the ceremony. The reciprocity of compliments between tea master and guest is a dance of civilities.

The tea gathering, called *chaj*, has many versions and parts. It lasts for a few hours, during which time a light meal with several courses is served, followed by *koicha*, which is thick green tea. The foods eaten represent the five basic tastes of salt, sweet, sour, bitter, and spice. The end of the ceremony is less formal and allows for easy bantering between guests.

Sweets are served with *usucha* or thin tea. Japanese tea ceremony sweets fall into two categories: the *namagashi* or moist sweets served before the thick tea, and the *higashi* or dry sweets served with thin tea. The latter resemble candies. It is this final part of the ceremony that is most easily re-created in your own home.

Steve Smith/Wheeler Pictures

Japanese temples are often the settings for the Chado *or tea ceremony.*

To set the scene, select a quiet room or cordon off a section with large, folding screens. Hang paper lanterns or balls to cover harsh light bulbs. Sparsely decorate the area with a few objects to capture the attention of your guests. A bonsai tree, reed flute, or Japanese lute (biwa) will garner compliments. The utensils used in the true tea ceremony are also quite beautiful and make charming centerpieces. A long-handled, thin, and austere bamboo water ladle, or split bamboo tea whisk, are works of art. The child's wooden horse is an ancient form of Japanese folk art, and the Japanese love for the elusive fish can be exhibited in a small tank of iridescent goldfish. In a slender vase, display singular stalks of flowers appropriate to the season: spring camellias or daffodils, summer iris, fall roses. If it is winter, hang a scroll of Japanese calligraphy. All decorative objects should be easily observed but unobtrusive.

There is a tremendous sense of order at a Japanese table setting. You will want a low, bare table with pillows to be used for seats. If you desire a table covering, use the bamboo mats designed for rolling sushi. On the mats place small, glazed dishes in red and black or earthy browns. If you prefer a pattern, look for something like the Japanese blue and white Imari ware sets which include teapots and cups. Or if you like, skip the china and serve the food on individual lacquered trays. Chopsticks should be placed in front of each diner, the thinner end pointing left and resting on a chopstick pillow. For napkins, use the traditional hand towels of Japan (tenugui) with graphically striking designs. You can also use them as runners on the table.

If possible, have a portable hot plate or brazier nearby, on which you place a kettle. Be sure the water is warm, not boiling. Rinse out and wipe each cup in front of your guests. Matcha, the powdered ceremonial green tea, should be whisked into a green froth and offered to the guests. If this tea is too bitter for

TEA IN JAPAN

Tea drinking in Japan starts at home in the morning and continues throughout the day at work and after hours with friends. Sometimes tea is taken in a special family room called the Chano-ma or tea room. The rice bowl has been dubbed the Chawan, or tea bowl, because of its important sidekick, tea. After a meal the Japanese tea drinker will occasionally pour very hot tea on rice left in this bowl. He will drink this with pickles, broiled salted salmon, or seafood preserves.

"Rice Tea"—a more formal variation of the occasional tea-drinker's habit—is often served after a meal but is customarily served at the end of the elaborate tea ceremony. Hot water is poured into the pot in which the rice was cooked. The boiled water loosens the remaining (usually burned) grains that flavor the liquid.

Green tea often accompanies portable lunches and snacks available in railroad stations, highway rest stops, temples, shrines, and restaurants. Moderate-sized cafeterias called Kissaten, which translates into "tea drinking shop," are popular cafes that provide a place for people from all walks of life to stop and chat. Bookshops have corner cafes where students and others meet to drink tea accompanied by small sandwiches and dishes of curried rice. A favorite lunch snack in Japan is Chazuke, a combination of fragrant green tea poured over rice with flaked fish and spices.

Although green tea is produced on a small scale, there are many varieties of it. The best leaves are Gyokuro, sold as "Pearl Dew." This tea has little tannic content so it tastes quite smooth and pleasant. Sencha is the most popular tea in the West and is the one you'll find in Japanese restaurants. Tencha or Matcha is the powdered tea used exclusively in the tea ceremony.

your taste, try *Gyokuro, Ocha,* or *Sencha.* Steep the leaves for two to three minutes in very hot (not boiling) water and pour into individual cups. It is considered improper to fill the cups more than two-thirds full, so pay constant attention to refill requests. With the bitter tea, serve the sweets that will balance the meal. Jellied red bean squares, rice-based confections, cooked chestnuts in sweetened syrup, sweet potatoes, and sweetened beans are popular. You can make them at home or buy them in a Japanese market. Garnishes are as important as the food. They are always elaborate but not ostentatious. Fruits and vegetables are shaped like flowers, swans, or foliage. You can have fun creating your own from lemon peels, carrots, dill, apples, and oranges.

If you prefer more substantial food, *Tenshin* is the more filling fare served at less formal tea ceremonies. Present your own version in a basket or lacquered box, and serve buckwheat noodles or sashimi with broiled fish, vegetables, pickles, and rice.

Michael Melford/Wheeler Pictures

Ceremonial green tea is prepared with special split bamboo whisks in a glazed bowl, above.

James Goslee III

A single yellow lily in a vase is typical of the austere settings designed for serene contemplation, left.

Sweet Jellied Red Bean Squares

An exotic taste sensation, these traditional Japanese sweets are to be taken with green tea. The sugared beans will surprise and delight the Western palate.

> 1/2 cup whole red azuki beans (or a 4 2/3-ounce bag), picked over, washed and drained (see note)
> 1 half-ounce package agar-agar strips, cut into 1/2-inch lengths (see note)
> 1 1/2 cups confectioner's sugar
> 2 tablespoons honey
> 2 tablespoons fresh, strained lemon juice
> (NOTE: Azuki beans and agar-agar are available at Japanese food shops and other specialty food stores, see appendix.)

Place beans and 3 cups water into heavy, medium-to large-size saucepan over high heat and bring to boil. Lower heat and simmer, uncovered, 2 minutes, stirring once. Bring to boil again, partially cover, leaving lid very slightly ajar. Stir, turn heat to low and simmer gently (water should have some bubbles) 45 minutes.

Meanwhile, into medium saucepan, place agar-agar and 1 1/2 cups cold water; soak 30 minutes. Place over moderate heat and bring to simmer. Cover, turn heat to low and simmer gently 5 to 8 minutes or until all the agar-agar has dissolved. Turn off heat and set aside.

Measure beans and their liquid. If necessary, add enough water to total 1 1/2 cups. Pour into blender or food processor and process until smooth paste is formed. Add sugar, honey, and lemon juice, blending after each addition (consistency and color will be like that of a dark chocolate sauce). Pour mixture back into saucepan and simmer over moderate heat to bubbling point. Turn heat to low and cook (there should be some bubbles), stirring constantly with wooden spoon, about 10 minutes until thick and creamy. Turn off heat.

Check to see if agar-agar is still hot; if not, heat over low 1 to 2 minutes. (Be sure to stir bean paste frequently so it does not burn.) Pour hot agar-agar into bean paste; mix well. Bring to simmer over moderate heat. Turn heat to low and cook, stirring constantly with wooden spoon, 15 minutes until mixture is thickened even more by agar-agar. Strain mixture into 8-inch square cake pan and cool completely until set. Cut with sharp knife into 1-inch squares.

Makes 42 squares.

Laura Ashley Dining Collection 1984

Chapter Five
TEA SERVICES AND ACCESSORIES

The earliest tea drinkers, the Chinese, did not use teapots, they boiled their leaves in kettlelike vessels. By the eighth century the Chinese drank tea from blue-glazed cups and their tea accoutrements started to resemble twentieth-century china. The first European cups were made in the manner of the handleless Chinese teacups. Tea was brewed in the cup and sipped from saucers. By the nineteenth century, the tea service had evolved into what we know today, including elaborate teapots. Soon sugar bowls, milk pitchers, and the paraphernalia needed to infuse the tea leaf became familiar teatime embellishments. The tea services and accessories we use today are a conglomeration of age-old designs and new, innovative shapes and colors.

Setting the Table

Teatime has no hard and fast rules of etiquette for table settings. You can use a perfectly matched set of china, or a mixture of "grandma's attic" cups and saucers. Of course, there should be enough elbow room, and the forks should be on the left, the knives on the right. Prepare the table to suit the mood of the occasion. You will need dinner plates for High Teas, and smaller salad-sized plates for less meal-oriented tea fare. Forks, knives, and spoons are a must. Teacups with matching saucers are standard, but mugs will provide a less formal setting. Remember sugar bowls, creamers, butter plates, and accessories for lemon slices, jam, and honey. The teapot is the main attraction, unless you are using a samovar or hot water urn. Finally, consider linens, candles, flowers, and other table top decorations.

Jeff McNamara

Susan M. Duane

Courtesy of Bing & Grondahl Inc.

Jeff McNamara

Inventiveness is the primary ingredient in a successful tea setting. Far left: A country table is enhanced by the blue check cloth that echoes the teapot's pattern. Top left: A picnic tea can include durable china such as this floral patterned cup, saucer, and pot. Left: Red flowers offset the dramatic black-and-white theme accented by the tablecloth, cow pitcher, teapot, and mugs. Top: Summer's simplicity is captured with a sunny peach on white china, ivory handled cutlery, and jacquard place mats and napkins all set on a bare wood table.

Tableware

China and Porcelain: This is fine pottery which originated in China and is now made all over the world. The best is thin, resists chipping, and has a translucent finish. It is used at a formal tea setting.

Stoneware and Earthenware: This is a more durable, thick pottery that is porous and soft enough to be easily scratched or chipped. It can be clay colored or glazed, often with a grayish tint. Use it for farm teas or casual gatherings. It mixes well with mugs or thick rimmed teacups.

Plastic and Paper: You can buy strong and attractive plastic plates for outdoor and Nursery Teas. Paper plates, if wax coated, are also a good choice for these occasions.

Courtesy of Villeroy & Boch

Here is an unusual pear-shaped china teapot.

© Harvey, Watkins, Senff

A contemporary service juxtaposes unusual angles.

Flatware is made of sterling silver, silver plate, and stainless steel. All are available in simple or elaborately carved patterns, with handles ranging from traditionally ornate English silver to wood, modern plastic in bright colors, or elegant and rarely seen ivory. While the gleam of a well polished silver is best suited to an elegant Victorian tea, almost any style is appropriate for most teas. The basic fork, knife, and teaspoon is all that you really need to set the tea, however, if you have butter knives and demitasse spoons for pots of jam, you can put them to good use. You might also need cake cutters and sharp knives for slicing meats at High Tea.

© Harvey, Watkins, Senit

A butterfly wing pattern is carried through with angular handles to create a zany patterned service.

"Peony" by Hermes for Robert Haviland

On a conventional yet distinctly bold china, bright flowers explode on a background pattern of pale green wicker, which gives the illusion of a porch or picnic setting.

Jeff McNamara

Seashore blues, golden sand, and the pastels of summer flowers can be found in glazed earthenware.

Teacups

The primary choices are dainty cups with handles, mugs, glasses in silver or plastic holders, or handleless bowls. Some people feel that tea is in its rightful place when served in traditional English bone china. Others prefer mugs because they hold more and bring warmth to cold hands. There are large cups with saucers, which also function as lids. The glass teacup is used in the Middle and Far East. It is advantageous if you want to show the rich, golden color of the tea infusion or if you have particularly lovely metal holders. The Orientals use small cups which fit well in the hand, and the design is as clean-looking and controlled as the ceremonies. Modern teacups come in unexpected shapes and colors.

For an alternative to the china cup, handpainted and glazed mugs inspire a jubilant atmosphere.

© Harvey, Watkins, Senft

Elyse Levin

Although blue and white are standard colors for china, this gold-rimmed setting with its unusual shape is decidedly more formal.

The green majolica plates are like petals supporting a red blossom (raspberry sorbet) and both colors are picked up in the Oriental-inspired china.

James R. Levin

Joe McNally/Wheeler Pictures

Pure white is a dignified classic and suggests an Eastern influence.

A selection of tea, individual hot water pots, and sterling silver strainers re-create a fancy English hotel tea.

Teapots and Tea Infusers

The teapot we use today is approximately the same as the one commonly used in the sixteenth century. Western teapots are made according to the original Chinese design. The seventeenth-century pots were made of silver, but most people agree that ceramic pots are more useful for keeping the tea warm.

You have a lot of choice when selecting a teapot because its shape has long inspired the creative touch of artists and inventors. There are silver, terra-cotta pottery, china, bone china, earthenware, ceramic, and glass teapots. For purposes of retaining heat and taste, it is best to avoid metal. However, if your priority is to add a touch of elegance to the table, a silver pot is perfect. Teapots can be original, one-of-a-kind designs which are handmade, or molded in the traditional pot-bellied, bell shapes. You can buy small, individual teapots for a setting, or use one big one. Some are designed with two compartments and spouts on either side for a choice of two teas or of having hot water on hand to weaken the brew. Fiestaware pots are lively with color and fun for informal tea gatherings. Memphis influenced craftsmen make teapots in brightly glazed ceramics with unexpected geometric shapes.

This pitcher, creamer, and teapot are perfect for a nursery tea.

The bold design of this tea set is reminiscent of the work of the design collaborative called Memphis.

© Harvey, Watkins, Senft

Rosenthal Studio-Linie

No matter what teapot you select, remember that its purpose is to keep the brewing water hot so that the leaves infuse quickly, and also to retain that heat so that the tea stays appropriately hot. Look for pots that will hold enough tea for the occasion, with spouts designed to pour easily without the danger of steam burning your hands or of unexpected drips. Be sure the lid fits securely in the opening so that it won't fall out when you are pouring the last of the tea. The best lids will have small lips which fit into the rim of the pot and hold it securely in place.

If you use loose tea you will probably put it straight into the pot, and when the tea is poured you will direct it through a strainer placed over the cup to catch the leaves from falling into the liquid. There are strainers designed to rest on the rim of the cup and tilt to the angle of the falling leaves. These are often silver, can be quite ornate, and are appropriate at a formal tea. However, the regular kitchen strainer with a handle will do for a less fancy setting.

Some teapots come with perforated infuser chambers which sit right in the center of the pot and can be removed once the tea has brewed. A new, enamel-lined kettle doubles as a teapot that can be brought directly to the table from the stovetop. Water is brought to a boil in the kettle which is then removed from the heat. A tea infuser basket full of tea is inserted for three to five minutes. Once removed, the tea can be served immediately. This avoids the step of pouring the water into the teapot, which causes the temperature to drop.

Another method of avoiding loose leaves in the tea is to use a metal tea ball or tea egg. Wire mesh infusers are the best because they allow a lot of water to circulate without releasing the leaves into the brew. The teaspoon infuser, a perforated spoon with a lid, is good for individual cups of tea.

The Design Council

Nothing is impossible. Teapots come in the shapes of rabbits, elephants, and even airplanes.

Tea Accoutrements

From tea in bed to tea at the fanciest table, trays will come in handy. For the formal tea choose silver trays. White wicker is nice for outdoor settings. Brass, lucite, teak, mahogany, lacquer, and plastic are some of the other choices. The designs range from rectangular with feet to round with a raised lip. Graduated sizes are nice for creating order in a hodgepodge of foods and china.

Cake stands are important for highlighting baked goods. They also add interesting levels to the table, drawing attention to the food. Tiered cake stands are traditional at teatime. They are a tidy way of presenting a lot of choices without cluttering the table. In the same vein, trolleys or rolling carts are good for displaying the lavish fare, organizing the dishes, and carrying things to and from the kitchen.

The Design Council

Linens can be elaborate or simple.

The Design Council

Place mats, napkins, and cozies are useful items.

Tea cozies make for a lively setting but can make tea bitter unless you remove the leaves from the pot.

Pop-up cards create a fantasy table setting.

Country-inspired china creates a relaxed setting.

Appendices
USEFUL NAMES AND ADDRESSES

Appendix One: Useful Names and Addresses

TEA ASSOCIATIONS

Tea Council of Canada
701 Evans Ave.
Suite 501
Etobicoke, Ontario M9C 1A3

Tea & Coffee Association of Canada
1185 Elinton Ave. East
Suite 101
Don Mills, Ontario M3C 3C6

Tea Council of the U.S.A.
230 Park Ave.
New York, NY 10169

Tea Board of India
445 Park Ave.
New York, NY 10022

United States Board of Tea Experts
Food & Drug Administration
850 Third Ave.
Brooklyn, NY 11232

Urasenke Tea Ceremony School
153 East 69th St.
New York, NY 10021

TEA PACKAGERS

Contact these companies for a complete listing of their blended and unblended teas, and their distributors. Some tea packagers even offer special tea caddies, gift packages, and other promotional items of interest.

Benchley Tea
RD #1 178–G
Highway 34 & Ridgewood Rd.
Wall Township, NJ 07719

R.C. Bigelow, Inc.
15 Merwin St.
Norwalk, CT 06856

Brooke Bond Oxo Ltd.
Leon House
High St.
Croydon, Surrey, England

Cadbury Typhoo Ltd.
Franklin House
P.O. Box 171
Bounville, Birmingham B30 2NA
England

Jacksons of Piccadilly
66–72 St. Johns Rd.
Clapham Junctions,
London SW11 1PT, England

Lyons Tetley Ltd.
325 Old Field Lande
Greenford, Middx UB6 0A8Z
England

Thomas J. Lipton, Inc.
800 Sylvan Ave.
Englewood Cliffs, NJ 07632

R. Twinings & Co., Ltd.
South Way
Andover, Hampshire SP10 5AQ
England

Celestial Seasonings (*Herbal Teas*)
1780 55th St.
Boulder, CO 80301-2795

TEA RETAILERS WITH
MAIL-ORDER SERVICES

American Tea, Coffee & Spice Co.
1511 Champa St.
Denver, CO 80202

Cambridge Coffee, Tea, and Spice House
1765 Massachussetts Ave.
Cambridge, MA 02138

Casa Moneo (*South American Maté*)
210 West 14th St.
New York, NY 10011

Crabtree & Evelyn
P.O. Box 187
Woodstock Hill, CT 02681

Empire Coffee & Tea
486 Ninth Ave.
New York, NY 10018

East India Tea and Coffee Co.
1481 Third St.
San Francisco, CA 94102

First Colony Coffee & Tea Co.
P.O. Box 11005
Norfolk, VA 23517

Gertrude H. Ford Tea Co.
P.O. Box 3407
110 Dutchess Turnpike
Poughkeepsie, NY 12603

Grace Tea Co., Ltd.
799 Broadway
New York, NY 10003

McNulty's Tea & Coffee Co.
109 Christopher St.
New York, NY 10014

Porto Rico Importing Co.
201 Bleecker St.
New York, NY 10012

Paprika Weiss
1546 Second Ave.
New York, NY 10028

H. Roth & Son
1577 First Ave.
New York, NY 10023

Schapira Coffee & Tea Co.
117 West 10th St.
New York, NY 10011

Star Bucks Coffee & Tea
c/o Peets Coffees
P.O. Box 8604
Emeryville, CA 94662

Williams Sonoma
576 Sutter St.
San Francisco, CA 94102

Zabars
2245 Broadway
New York, NY 10024

Appendix Two: State-by-State Gourmet Mail-Order Guide

CALIFORNIA

Ai Hoa Market (*Japanese*)
860 North Hill St.
Los Angeles, CA 90012

Asia Food Market (*Japanese*)
2000 Judah St.
San Francisco, CA 94122

Bazaar of India (*Indian*)
1131 University Ave.
Berkeley, CA 94702

Berjian Grocery (*Indian*)
4725 Santa Monica Blvd.
Los Angeles, CA 90029

The Chinese Grocer (*Chinese*)
209 Post St.
San Francisco, CA 94108

Haig's Delicacies (*Middle Eastern*)
441 Clement St.
San Francisco, CA 94118

International Food (*Russian*)
7754 Santa Monica Blvd.
Los Angeles, CA 90046

Kwa On Lung Co. (*Chinese*)
686 North Spring St.
Los Angeles, CA 90015

Ron's Supermarket (*Russian*)
5270 Sunset Blvd.
Hollywood, CA 90027

CONNECTICUT

Dimyan's Market (*Middle Eastern*)
116 Elm St.
Danbury, CT 06810

India Health Foods (*Indian*)
1161 State St.
Bridgeport, CT 06605

COLORADO

Pacific Mercantile Grocery (*Japanese*)
1925 Lawrence St.
Denver, CO 80202

WASHINGTON, DC

Skenderis Gree Import (*Middle Eastern*)
1612 20 St. NW
Washington, DC 20009

Spices & Foods Unlimited
2018A Florida NW
Washington, DC 20009

FLORIDA

South And Eastern Food Supply (*Chinese*)
6732 NE Fourth Ave.
Miami, FL 33138

GEORGIA

Asian Supermarket (*Japanese*)
2581 Piedmont Rd.
Atlanta, GA 30324

ILLINOIS

Far East Trading Co. (*Japanese*)
2837 North Western Ave.
Chicago, IL 60618

INDIANA

A.B. Oriental Grocery (*Chinese*)
3707 Suit Shadeland Ave.
Indianapolis, IN 46226

Athens Imported Food (*Middle Eastern*)
City Market 84–85
Indianapolis, IN 46204

LOUISIANA

Korea House (*Japanese*)
615 Orange St.
New Orleans, LA 70130

MAINE

Model Food Importers
(*Middle Eastern*)
113–115 Middle St.
Portland, ME 04101

MARYLAND

Asia House Grocery (*Chinese*)
2433 Saint Paul St.
Baltimore, MD 21218

MASSACHUSSETTS

Cardullo's Gourmet Shop (*Middle Eastern*)
6 Brattle St.
Cambridge, MA 02138

Syrian Grocery Import Co.
(*Middle Eastern*)
270 Shawmut Ave.
Boston, MA 02118

Yoshinoya (*Japanese*)
36 Prospect St.
Cambridge, MA 02139

NEW JERSEY

Shop and Save (*Russian*)
1244 Hamilton Ave.
Trenton, NJ 08629

NEW YORK

Annapurna (*Indian*)
127 East 28th St.
New York, NY 10016

Carnig Tashjian
(*Middle Eastern*)
380 Third Ave.
New York, NY 10016

Gold Star Trading Co. (*Russian*)
570 Smith St.
Brooklyn, NY 11231

Katagiri Co. (*Japanese*)
224 East 59th St.
New York, NY 10022

Lee's Oriental Gifts & Foods (*Chinese*)
3053 Main St.
Buffalo, NY 14214

Little India Store (*Indian*)
128 East 28th St.
New York, NY 10016

Kam Man Food Products (*Chinese*)
200 Canal St.
New York, NY 10013

Paprika Weiss (*Russian*)
1546 Second Ave.
New York, NY 10028

H. Roth & Son (*Russian*)
1577 First Ave.
New York, NY 10023

Tanaka And Co. (*Japanese*)
326 Amsterdam Ave.
New York, NY 10023

Wing Fat Co., Inc. (*Chinese*)
33–35 Mott St.
New York, NY 10013

Wing Woh Lung Co. (*Chinese*)
50 Mott St.
New York, NY 10013

OHIO

Far East Co. (*Chinese*)
247 West McMillin St.
Cincinnati, OH 45219

PENNSYLVANIA

Harmony Oriental (*Chinese*)
247 Atwood St.
Pittsburgh, PA 15213

India Food Mart (*Indian*)
808 South 47 St.
Philadelphia, PA 19143

International Mini Market (*Russian*)
10185 Veree Rd.
Philadelphia, PA 19116

TEXAS

Antones Import Co. (*Indian*)
4234 Harry Hines Blvd.
Dallas, TX 75219

WASHINGTON

Uwajimaya (*Chinese/Japanese*)
P.O. Box 3003
Seattle, WA 98114

CANADA

Mihamaya (*Japanese*)
392 Powell St.
Vancouver, Br. Columbia
Canada,VGA 1G4

Top Banana Ltd. (*Indian*)
1526 Merivale Rd.
Ottawa, Ontario
Canada, K2G 3JS

Index